D0445907

HOW (NOT) TO SPEAK
OF GOD

HOW (NOT) TO SPEAK OF GOD

Peter Rollins

PARACLETE PRESS
BREWSTER, MASSACHUSETTS

How (Not) to Speak of God

2008 Second Printing
2006 First Printing

ISBN: 978-1-55725-505-1

This edition published by Paraclete Press, 2006.
First published in Great Britain in 2006 by
Society for Promoting Christian Knowledge
36 Causton Street
London SW1P 4ST

3 5 7 9 10 8 6 4 2

Typeset by Graphicraft Ltd, Hong Kong

Published by Paraclete Press
Brewster, Massachusetts
www.paracletepress.com

Printed in the United States of America

To the Menagerie

For you opened your doors to us

Contents

Acknowledgements

———◦•◦———

Books are authored by countless people and credited to only one. They each represent little kingdoms of thought built from the toil of others that gratify the tiny tyrant who chained the disparate ideas together. If I were to begin to thank all those who have helped to steer my thinking, it would be a long list. With that in mind, I will stick to thanking those who were directly involved with encouraging me in this particular work. My thanks go to Ian Mitchell, the one who said that I ought to publish a book on this subject; Alison Barr, who opened up the way for it to be published; and Andrew King and Cary Gibson, who helped render the material publishable. My deep thanks also go to Brian McLaren, Phyllis Tickle, Jonny Baker, Helena Macormac, the Ikon 'cyndicate', Francie and my parents.

Foreword

———◆———

I am a raving fan of the book you are holding. I loved reading it. I have already begun widely recommending it. In the last two days I have recommended it to three rabbis, and in recent weeks, to many Christian leaders. Reading it did good for my mind and for my soul. It helped me understand my own spiritual journey more clearly, and it gave me a sense of context for the work I'm involved in. It drew unexpected connections – between the medieval Christian mystics and contemporary philosophy, for example, and it stirred my imagination. In fact, I would say this is one of the two or three most rewarding books of theology I have read in ten years. Do I sound like I'm raving yet?

My enthusiasm is all the more significant because I read a lot of theology. To me, nothing (or almost nothing) is more elevating and challenging, yet more humbling and overwhelming, than setting the mind to think about God, and to think about thinking and speaking about God. I am nearly always working through a work of theology, either ancient or contemporary. So when I say this book is among the best I've read, I'm saying something significant.

And it's more significant still because the author of this book is a young – and I think it's safe to say up-until-now *unknown* – emerging theologian. But as this book makes clear, he deserves to be known and appreciated, especially when one thinks that this may be the first of many contributions he makes in the years to come.

Growing up in Belfast, Northern Ireland, Peter Rollins has seen Christianity expressed in one of its more dysfunctional Western forms where the division between Protestants and Catholics frequently has gone bloody, hateful, and bitter. Speaking of God in Northern Ireland has too often fomented distrust and prejudice, not peace and reconciliation: speaking of God has too often been part of the problem, not of the solution. Like a kid growing up in a conflicted family characterized by loud and violent fights with the windows wide open, he has had to grapple with issues that more genteel dysfunctional families can more successfully hide. His setting prepares him uniquely to speak about how (not) to speak for God – and one hopes that people in other settings will learn much from him, including my own conflicted country.

Coming of age in what is often called a postmodern context, Peter Rollins was not formed – at least not successfully – within the constraints of modernity. He represents what is to me one of the first and most hopeful expressions to date of Christian theology being done in a postmodern context – not merely speaking of postmodernity in the context of theology, but speaking of God meaningfully in the context of postmodernity. Some have said that theology in the context of postmodernity is impossible or unfruitful, but here they will see better (im)possibilities. Again and again, Peter challenges us to embrace opposite ends of common modern polarities, and, in so doing, shows the creative and constructive power of what is commonly called *deconstruction*.

Equally unusual and significant, Peter is doing the serious work of theology while rooted more in a faith community than in an academic institution. As the second part of the book makes clear, Peter believes that people who are engaged in real communities of spiritual practice are uniquely prepared to speak of God. The rituals and gatherings of the Ikon community may be uncomfortable to some, even as they prove inspiring and moving to others.

I know I winced on one occasion as I imagined participating in some elements of the liturgies that were described. If we find ourselves offended or disturbed by elements of the Ikon services, we might ask ourselves whether the disruption of a disturbing liturgy is necessary at times to arouse people like us from the religious slumbers that so frequently overtake us – like the bizarre characters in a Flannery O'Connor novel or short story, for example – to jolt us into the realization that we routinely tolerate the intolerable in the ways we speak of God. Could there be some resonance here with the disturbing actions taken by some of the biblical prophets – like Isaiah preaching naked for three years, Ezekiel cooking his food over excrement, or Hosea marrying a woman of ill repute – actions whose very oddness disrupts business as usual in the ways we speak of God?

Peter includes them not so that others will imitate them as a 'mass-reproducible model', but so that the reader can imagine what this way of (not) speaking of God looks like as practised in one innovative faith community in one storied location at one important historical moment. One hopes that many others will be inspired to appropriate creativity in their situations.

Not many who speak of God do so in ways that are at one moment deeply inspiring and poignant in resonance with the great Christian mystics and, at the next, disturbing in the tradition of the Hebrew prophets. Not many people who speak of God do so with a mixture of Pentecostal/Evangelical experience, a wide reading in Christian devotional literature, and a thoughtful engagement with postmodern philosophical scholarship. Peter does.

Add to all these rare qualities one more: Peter's strong talent for turning a phrase. In the coming pages you will encounter freshly worded insights like these: colonizing the 'name' of God with concepts ... the brutality of words ... believing the right way ... God's omni-nameability ... theism, atheism, antitheism, and a/theism ... hyper-presence ... the God-shaped hole ... consumption and condemnation ... a transfinite set of interpretations. If you're like me, you'll find yourself underlining and marking page after page, grateful for not only the stimulating ideas, but for their lucid expression. And Peter's effective and creative use of parables comes as an added surprise, evoking the practice of a communicator who, many of us believe, spoke of God as no other person ever has, to such a degree that he himself was named the Word made flesh.

I share Peter's enthusiasm for what he calls 'the emergent conversation'. Here he makes one of the most important contributions to date to that conversation. I hope that what he says here will draw more and more people into that conversation – including people who will charitably, respectfully and responsibly challenge some of his ideas. In this way, both he and they will give us all more to think and speak about. As Peter says, 'That which we cannot speak of is the one thing about whom and to whom we must never stop speaking.'

All in the emergent community share the hope that our ongoing conversation about and with God will prove converting and transformative for all of us who participate, and for our faith communities, and for our world. Many will share my enthusiasm about this book and my gratitude to – and for – its author.

Brian D. McLaren
(www.anewkindofchristian.com, www.amahoro.info)

Introduction

The secret

---•◆•---

That which one writes last is read first. As such, the introduction of a book is really the author's conclusion, a way of looking over the ground that has been traversed and expressing the overall trajectory of the journey. Looking over what I have written, I find myself wondering once more why I have chosen the subject of God. After all, this area must be among the most difficult and dangerous of them all. So much ink has been spent in writing of God and so much blood has been spilt in the name of God that I shudder each time I think about writing on the subject. Because of this concern I have often found myself drawn to the sentiment expressed by the philosopher Ludwig Wittgenstein in the final sentence of his influential *Tractatus Logico-Philosophicus*:

> What we cannot speak about we must pass over in silence.[1]

Time and again I have found great wisdom in this phrase, and yet I have not left these pages blank. Perhaps part of the reason why I find myself unable to stay silent derives from the fact that long before I ever came across this sentiment, I had become deeply involved with the evangelical charismatic movement. Here I learnt a very different type of wisdom, one that I have never been able to shake. In short it was this:

> God is the one subject of whom we must never stop speaking.

At first these two approaches seemed like oil and water, yet I could not completely reject either. When the philosophical subtlety of the former gained power, I would find myself tempted toward a mystical humanism; and when the passion of the latter gained a stronger grip, I started a slide in the direction of religious fundamentalism.

Yet, in the midst of this tug of war, I began to feel that these positions need not be enemies. The more I reflected upon the depth of these perspectives, the more I began to suspect that, far from being utterly foreign to each other, there was a way in which they could inform and enrich each other. More than this, I began to suspect that such a dialogue between these two positions not only could be personally liberating but also could unleash an approach to faith that might help to revitalize the Western Church.

Yet the question remained as to what this dialogue would look like, for each time I reflected on the positions, I was struck by their seemingly exclusive and all-embracing nature. While Wittgenstein's God was an unbreakable secret that could not be shared, to contemporary evangelicals God was one who had broken this secrecy and thus needed to be shared.

Each time I returned to the horns of this dilemma, I found myself drawn to the Christian mystics (such as Meister Eckhart), for while they did not embrace total silence, they balked at the presumption of those who would seek to colonize the name 'God' with concepts. Instead of viewing the unspeakable as that which brings all language to a halt, they realized that the unspeakable was precisely the place where the most inspiring language began. This God whose name was above every name gave birth, not to a poverty of words, but to an excess of them. And so they wrote elegantly concerning the limits of writing and spoke eloquently about the brutality of words. By speaking with wounded words of their wounded Christ, these mystics helped to develop, not a distinct religious tradition, but rather a way of engaging with and understanding already existing religious traditions: seeing them as a loving response to God rather than a way of defining God.

In these often overlooked writings I discovered a way to embrace both the wisdom of those who would say that God is unspeakable, and must therefore be passed over in silence, and the wisdom of those who would say that God can, and must, be expressed. The union can be articulated like this:

That which we cannot speak of is the one thing about whom and to whom we must never stop speaking.

For the mystic God was neither an unspeakable secret to be passed over in silence, nor a dissipated secret that had been laid bare in revelation. Rather, the mystic approached God as a secret which one was compelled to share, yet which retained its secrecy.

By the late medieval period this perspective was largely drowned out by the approach of theologians such as Duns Scotus, and it remained on the sidelines of faith throughout modernity (I am thinking here primarily of the influence of Cartesian thought). Even today, when I looked around, it seemed that the mystical approach was being either ignored by the wider Christian community or viewed as a private practice to be engaged in during remote weekend retreats. The only people who seemed to be taking this subject seriously were the supposedly nihilistic postmodern philosophers. Yet the more I studied this discourse, the more I returned to the view that this lost language was among the most stunning, sophisticated and simple ways of approaching faith. It became clear to me that for the Western Church to prosper in the twenty-first century, it needed to engage with this ancient language.[2] It was in light of this that I set about writing *How (Not) To Speak of God*.

The work itself is made up of two quite different though complementary parts. Part 1 draws from my experience as an academic and introduces some of the theoretical background for this type of thinking. Chapter 1 explores the nature of revelation and argues that, far from being the opposite of concealment, the Word of God has mystery built into its very heart. Chapter 2 builds upon this insight by exploring how such thinking critiques the idea of theology as that which speaks of God in favour of the idea that theology is the place where God speaks. Against the idea that we can speak of God I argue that we must embrace an a/theological approach that acknowledges the extent to which our supposed God-talk fails to define who or what God is. Chapter 3 delves deeper into these issues by exploring how this a/theology is not divorced from God but rather is a response to the work of God and a means of approaching God. Chapter 4 explores how the rediscovery of mystery, doubt, complexity and ambiguity in faith helps us come to a more appropriate understanding of religious desire, while Chapter 5 draws out the centrality of love in Christian thinking.

Part 2 draws upon my experience as founder and active participant in a group called 'Ikon'. Ikon was originally an experimental
project dedicated to exploring the relationship between mysticism
and postmodern thought in a liturgical context and has since
developed into an important model for those who are seeking to
rethink the structure of religious communities in a contemporary
environment. Ikon's main event takes place in Belfast once a
month in a pub called The Menagerie and is attended by a range
of people spanning the liberal/conservative, protestant/catholic
and theist/atheist divides. The services themselves can be described
as a form of 'theodrama' insomuch as they employ a cocktail of live
art, poetry, prose, ritual, liturgy and music so as to immerse the individual in a sensually rich environment that is designed to draw out
an openness to the incoming of God.

Part 2 is composed of a brief description of ten Ikon services. Each
chapter offers a background to the particular evening and an outline
of what transpired. Part 2 is designed to offer some examples of
how one group has explored, within a liturgical context, the theory
discussed in Part 1. The hope is not that people will reconstruct these
services in their entirety (although everyone is welcome to do so) but
rather that, by describing some of the ways that we have approached
the issues, these outlines will be a type of springboard that will
enable others to create more inspiring, challenging and provocative
services than we have as yet been able to imagine.

The book as a whole is aimed at either those already involved in
what has been called 'the emerging conversation' or those who
would like to understand it in a deeper way. The reason for my interest in this diverse network derives from the fact that it is here where
I have been lucky enough to encounter others on a similar quest as
myself. Indeed, it is in the fruits of this conversation that I see real
hope for a robust, challenging and inspirational form of Christianity,
one with roots in the past, a sensitivity to the present and a vision
for the future. The term 'emerging Church' has also been used to
describe this diverse community. While it is a useful term, the word
'Church' can be quite misleading, since the movement is not so
much developing a distinct religious tradition within Christianity,
but rather is re-introducing ideas that help to both revitalize already

existing religious traditions and build bridges between them. It is not then a revolution that is in the process of creating something new but rather one that is returning to something very old. It is here that I am reminded of G. K. Chesterton when he wrote of a desire to one day pen a story that tells of an English yachtsman who miscalculated his journey and returned to England with the belief that he had discovered a new land. On sharing this idea, he writes:

> There will probably be a general impression that the man who landed (armed to the teeth and talking by signs) to plant a British flag on that barbaric temple which turned out to be the Pavilion at Brighton, felt rather a fool. I am not here concerned to deny that he looked like a fool. But if you imagine that he felt like a fool, or at any rate that the sense of folly was his sole or his dominant emotion, then you have not studied with sufficient delicacy the rich romantic nature of the hero of this tale.[3]

The hero of Chesterton's allegory overcomes any sense of foolishness with a profound joy, as he is in a unique position to experience the wonder and fear associated with discovering something new alongside the comfort and security of having come home.

The energy and vitality that exists within the emerging conversation is exhilarating, and at times it seems as if those involved are charting a new direction for Christianity. Yet time and again familiar sounding place names gently remind us that this discovery is at the same time a re-discovery. I began this introduction with the comment that it is really my conclusion, and my conclusion is this: the territory I thought I was helping to chart was actually discovered a long time ago by my ancestors. It is both frustrating and comforting that no matter how fast I run, those who have long since died have already arrived at where I am attempting to go.

Peter Rollins

Part 1

HERETICAL ORTHODOXY: FROM RIGHT BELIEF TO BELIEVING IN THE RIGHT WAY

Christian faith, it could be said, is born in the aftermath of God. Our fragile faith is fanned into life in the wake of what we believe to have been the incoming of a life-giving encounter in which we feel connected with, and transformed by, the source of everything that is. This belief may result from an immediate and psychologically penetrating experience or may arise more gently over time, but, regardless of the means, such faith cannot be reduced to the mere affirmation of religious dogma, a regular visit to some religious institution or the reciting of mechanical prayers. For Christians testify to having been caught up in and engulfed by that which utterly transcends them. In short, the experience that gives birth to faith, at its most luminous, is analogous to the experience of an infant feeling the embrace and tender kiss of its mother.

On the other hand, theology could be provisionally described as that which attempts to come to grips with this life-giving experience, to describe the source from which everything is suspended and from which our faith is born. In faith God is experienced as the absolute subject who grasps us, while in theology we set about reflecting upon this subject. Here the source of our desire is rendered into an

1

(intellectual) object that we may reflect upon. In faith we are held, in theology we hold.

Faith and theology, in this reading, seem inextricably intertwined, as there can be no experience of faith divorced from an interpretation of it. Indeed, Christianity without theology could never really be 'Christian', for the term presupposes that one interprets the encounter with God in relation to the Judeo-Christian scriptures. According to this logic, theology, in its modern form, has been concerned with upholding and defending the notion of orthodoxy as that which articulates a correct understanding of God.

Yet the idea that we may understand the source of faith in this way has been roundly attacked both by those outside the Church and by those within it. The argument is made that naming God is never really naming God but only naming our understanding of God. To take our ideas of the divine and hold them as if they correspond to the reality of God is thus to construct a conceptual idol built from the materials of our mind.

In Part 1 I explore how the contemporary Church has been unable to take on this insight and is thus always in danger of intellectual idolatry. I also argue that the liberal religious community is caught in a similar bind, for by taking these critiques on board they have mistakenly given up on the idea that we can speak meaningfully of God at all. While one side naïvely claims that orthodoxy (as right belief) is still possible, the other counters that all we can ever affirm about God is heretical. While one affirms the supremacy of their God in an implicitly exclusive and violent way, the other reduces faith to a purely immanent ethical system.

In contrast to this, I argue here that those involved in the emerging conversation exhibit the conceptual tools that are necessary to move beyond these modernistic and problematic positions. Here I picture the emerging community as a significant part of a wider religious movement which rejects both absolutism and relativism as idolatrous positions which hide their human origins in the modern myth of pure reason. Instead of following the Greek-influenced idea of orthodoxy as right belief, these chapters show that the emerging community is helping us to rediscover the more Hebraic and mystical notion of the orthodox Christian as one who believes in the right way – that is, believing in a loving, sacrificial and Christlike manner. The reversal from 'right belief' to 'believing in the right way' is in no way a move to some binary opposite of the first (for the opposite of right belief is simply wrong belief); rather, it is a way transcending the binary altogether. Thus orthodoxy is no longer (mis)understood as the opposite of heresy but rather is understood as a term that signals a way of being in the world rather than a means of believing things about the world.

As we shall see, this approach opens up a Christian thinking that profoundly challenges some of the most basic ideas found in the contemporary Church. It is an approach which emphasizes the priority of love: not as something which stands opposed to knowledge of God, or even as simply more important than knowledge of God, but, more radically still, *as* knowledge of God.

To love is to know God precisely because God is love. The emerging community, at its best, can teach us again that love must be the first word on our lips and also the last, and that we must seek to incarnate that sacred word in the world. I recently heard a well-known speaker say that if faith does not cost us something, then it is nothing. Only much later could I respond: if faith does not cost us everything, it is nothing. Orthodoxy as right belief will cost us little; indeed, it will allow us to sit back with our Pharisaic doctrines, guarding the 'truth' with the purity of our interpretations. But orthodoxy, as believing in the right way, as bringing love to the world around us and within us . . . that will cost us everything. For to live by that sword, as we all know, is to die by it.

Chapter 1

God rid me of God

◆◈◆

Away-from-here

While the term 'emerging Church' is increasingly being employed to describe a well-defined and well-equipped religious movement, in actual fact it is currently little more than a fragile, embryonic and diverse conversation being held between individuals over the Internet and at various small gatherings. Not only does the elusive and tentative nature of this conversation initially make it difficult to describe what, if anything, unifies those involved; the sheer breadth of perspectives held by those within the dialogue makes terms such as 'movement', 'denomination' and 'church' seem somehow inappropriate.

Our first attempt to understand this network will often leave us with a certain frustration, as its kinetic and dynamic nature seems to defy easy reduction to a single set of theological doctrines or ritualistic practices. What we are presented with instead is a diverse matrix of relationships that bridge a number of different communities. Even a cursory glance over this network will show that the participants are unified neither by a shared theological tradition, nor by an aspiration to one day develop one. The word 'emerging' cannot, then, be understood as describing a type of becoming that is set to one day burst onto the religious scene as a single, unified and distinct denominational perspective (analogous to a caterpillar that is soon to break its cocoon and arise as a butterfly), or a becoming that can be carefully charted (like the trajectory of a bullet).

However, the word 'emerging' is not arbitrary, for it does help us to identify some kind of initial unity. On closer inspection we find that there is a sense in which those involved in the conversation acknowledge that Christianity involves a process of journeying and becoming. There is a shared understanding that *being* a Christian always involves *becoming* a Christian. This may seem like a rather mundane insight until it is juxtaposed with some prevalent ideas that surround us. We need not look far to find that our religious communities, influenced as they are by the movement known as modernity, have tended to emphasize the idea of 'being' and 'destination': one *becomes* a Christian, *joins* a church and *is* saved. From this idea of destination flows our understanding of evangelism as a means of sharing our faith and encouraging others to embrace it for themselves. For those involved in the emerging conversation, this view distorts the deeper meaning of evangelism, for once we acknowledge that we are *becoming* Christian, *becoming* Church and *being* saved, then the other can be seen as a possible instrument of our further conversion. Even a brief reflection upon the darkness in our own lives bears testimony to the fact that we need to be evangelized as much, if not more, than those around us.

This is not to say that those involved in the emerging conversation choose the idea of journeying over and above the idea of destination; rather, there is a sense in which such binary thinking is rejected in favour of the view that faith embraces journey as a type of destination. We can see an example of this seemingly paradoxical path in the parable of a young traveller who is busy preparing his horse for a long and arduous journey. As he packs his few possessions an old friend approaches and asks, 'Where are you going?' Without looking up, the traveller quietly replies, 'Away from here.' After a short pause his friend repeats the question, and again the traveller responds by saying, 'I am going away from here.' Finally the friend exclaims, 'I already know that you are leaving us, but what is your destination?' In response the traveller stops what he is doing and looks directly into the eyes of his companion. 'I have already told you my destination, dear friend. It is *away-from-here.*'

A revolution of the 'how'

Yet it would be a mistake to think that the only thing which unifies this fragile network is the shared commitment to understanding faith as a process, for this conversation offers the potential of a dramatic revolution in religious thought. While most religious revolutions are instigated by people who seek to offer answers to questions which they believe the denomination they are a part of is unable, unwilling or ill equipped to answer (thus setting up a new denomination), this revolution is of a fundamentally different and deeper kind.

Unlike those who would seek to offer a different set of answers to theological questions, those within the emerging conversation are offering a different way of understanding the answers that we already possess. In other words, those involved in the conversation are not explicitly attempting to construct or unearth a different set of beliefs that would somehow be more appropriate in today's context, but rather, they are looking at the way in which we hold the beliefs that we already have. This is not then a revolution that seeks to change what we believe, but rather one that sets about transforming the entire manner in which we hold our beliefs. In short, this revolution is not one which merely adds to or subtracts from the world of our understanding, but rather one which provides the necessary tools for us to be able to look at that world in a completely different manner: in a sense, nothing changes and yet the shift is so radical that absolutely nothing will be left unchanged.

Speaking (of) God

Christianity is generally accepted to rest upon the belief that God has communicated with humanity via revelation. There is then what some philosophers call the affirmation of an underlying 'ontology of participation', meaning that Christianity is premised upon the idea that there is a connection between the creation and the creator. Yet beyond this rather general affirmation concerning the existence of revelation there is the question of how we come to understand this revelation. For the contemporary Church the answer basically boils down to this: *revelation is that which reveals*. In other words, Christianity, as that which is brought into being and maintained by revelation, has a privileged access to the mind of God. Revelation is thus understood to be the very opposite of concealment. It is argued that if God's communication to humanity is to mean anything at all, it must mean precisely what it infers: that God has graciously disclosed something of God's nature to us. In this rendering, theology, as the discipline that systematically reflects upon revelation, is understood as the science that places God within the realm of reason.[4] This view is further supported by the fact that the word 'theology' is derived from the Greek terms *theos* (meaning God) and *logos* (referring to reason or word).

Revelation against concealment

Yet the view that revelation is the opposite of concealment, far from being obvious, self-evident and timeless, actually owes much of its contemporary currency to the philosophical thought that gained dominance during the Enlightenment.[5] This period was also known as the Age of Reason and was a time when many thinkers rejected the scholastic philosophy which defined the thought of the Middle Ages (a type of thinking that was perceived as mired by superstition and constrained by religious authority) in favour of systems based upon the employment of pure reason. For an Enlightenment thinker, beliefs were to be based upon clear thinking and solid rational foundations rather than custom, authority or instinct. The general philosophical climate at that time was one of deep suspicion concerning any claims that were based upon revelation and the authority of religious institutions.

Although the anti-ecclesiastical slant of the time was largely rejected by the Church and many theologians wished to retain the centrality of revelation, they eagerly embraced the Enlightenment's high regard concerning reason. And so, while explicitly opposing the secularization of the time, they ended up mirroring its underlying presuppositions. The dominant thinking within both the universities and the Church accepted that humans had a capacity to grasp objective, universal truth. Whether it was the painstaking empirical work of the natural scientist, the positivist research of the social scientist or the hermeneutic approach to scripture engaged in by the theologian, it was believed that, by employing pure reason (reason untouched by prejudice) one could decipher the *singular* meaning of what was being studied (whether it be the natural world or a supernatural revelation).[6] Just as the scientist believed that the world was something that could be understood through the application of reason, so the theologian believed that God was open to our understanding insomuch as God was revealed to us through the scriptures. While it was readily accepted that much of God still lay in inaccessible darkness, it was claimed that what God revealed through nature, the prophets and Christ was clearly manifest to us precisely because God had spoken there.

The end of ideology

Yet by the end of the nineteenth century and the beginning of the twentieth, the idea of a neutral, disinterested space within which reason could operate without underlying influences (the ideal of secularism) was placed into serious question by such perceptive thinkers as Feuerbach, Nietzsche, Marx and Freud, each of whom explored the extent to which our supposedly objective understanding of the world or God is always already affected by such factors as our education, upbringing, economic position and psychological makeup. These thinkers persuasively uncovered the various places in which our supposedly untainted, objective and rational understanding of the world or God was influenced by a variety of largely subconscious, self-interested desires.[7] In doing so they each helped to point out that when we make absolute claims concerning what we believe about the world or God, acting as if our opinions were the result of some painstaking, objective and rational reflection, we end up deceiving ourselves, for our understanding is always an interpretation of the information before us (whether the raw material of the world or revelation) and thus is always affected by what we bring to the table. For instance, in the image below, we will see either a duck or a rabbit but not both at the same time. Neither will we be able to see the lines of the picture devoid of one of these images. In

a similar way, we can say that we never see the world as it really is (as symbolized by the lines) but always place meaning onto it (symbolized by the duck or rabbit).

This approach has been called the 'critique of ideology' because of the way that it questions the extent to which any existing understanding of the world is able to really express anything objective about how the world really is. The term 'ideology' refers to any system which is held as a verbal representation of how things really are. It is derived from the Greek terms *eidos* (meaning the essential core) and *logos* (reason).

In the aftermath of these deconstructive thinkers, it was virtually impossible to think critically about the world without acknowledging that our views have been influenced by such factors as our cultural tradition, biological traits, unconscious libidinal desires and economic position. The overall result of this genealogical critique was a radical undermining of any system that declared absolute authority by claiming to somehow reveal God or expose Ultimate Meaning to the clear light of day.

In the wake of these thinkers many have claimed that the only way to think about reality is in terms of a human construct that is formed purely from a complex network of social interactions. Indeed Nietzsche, Marx and Freud have often been (mis)used in order to justify a form of nihilism which claims that the universe arose from nothing, is going nowhere and possesses no meaning. This has led to two dominant reactions by the Western Church. First, the predominant response has been by those who would close their ears to such critiques and run back to the naïveté that existed before these great iconoclasts came onto the scene. Second, there has been the less popular but deeply influential response of those who claim that we must bite the bullet and forge a new Christianity from the carcass of the old, a Christianity that is concerned with developing an ethical way of life based on the teachings of Jesus while rejecting the question of God as an irrelevant abstraction belonging to the past.

Although these two approaches appear to operate at opposite ends of the conceptual spectrum, they both mistakenly agree that if one accepts the idea that all our theological constructions are deeply tainted by the limits of our intelligence, the influence of our culture and the unfathomable workings of our subconscious desires, then one must necessarily give up on a meaningful faith.

Beyond meaning and meaninglessness

However, such a view fundamentally misses the point that, once we give up on the idea that we can make objective, meaningful statements, we must also give up the possibility of making any nihilistic claims concerning the meaninglessness of the world. Here we can begin to perceive one of the central elements of the postmodern critique, namely the recognition that relativism (i.e. the claim that there is no meaning) is ultimately self-contradictory, for to say that there is no meaning to the universe is itself a meaningful statement, as it makes a meaningful claim about the way that the universe really is. Hence relativism is inherently self-contradictory and devours itself.

The idea of an objective world was not rejected by these great 'masters of suspicion' (a title bestowed upon Nietzsche, Freud and Marx), only the idea that human beings could grasp this objective world in an objective manner. Like the duck/rabbit diagram above, we can still talk of a real world: it is just that we can never see it in an unadulterated manner because, as interpretive beings, we always filter the real world through our experiences, language, intelligence, culture and so forth.

The idolatry of ideology

It is here that those involved in the emerging conversation are able to cut a path beyond these two dead ends, a way that embraces the critique of ideology as reflected in a profoundly religious approach to be found both in the Bible and in later Christian tradition. One of the primary reasons why the emerging community can embrace the work of God while acknowledging the critique of ideology, rather than rejecting it as an enemy or accepting it as the necessary end of all claims concerning God, lies precisely in the fact that the philosophical critique of ideology mirrors the biblical rejection of idolatry.

This relation between the trespass of idolatry and the critique of ideology becomes clearer when we note that the word 'idolatry', like 'ideology', also derives from the Greek term *eidos* (meaning essence). This helps us get to the heart of what idolatry actually is. The term can be understood to refer to any attempt that would render the essence of God accessible, bringing God into either aesthetic visibility (in the form of a physical structure, such as a statue) or conceptual visibility (in the form of a concept, such as a theological system). Like an aesthetic idol (such as the Golden Calf in the book of Exodus), the conceptual idol refers to any system of thought which the individual or community takes to be a visible rendering of God. The only significant difference between the aesthetic idol and the conceptual idol lies in the fact that the former reduces God to a physical object while the latter reduces God to an intellectual object.

Idolatry does not rest in the idea of the object itself but rather in the eye of the beholder. In other words, it is the way one engages with an object or idea that makes an idol an idol rather than some kind of property within it. For instance, in the past many Romans would have perceived a statue of Apollo as the visible representation of a divinity, while today we appreciate it purely as a sculpture or ancient artefact.

The Bible and conceptual idolatry

This idea of conceptual idolatry is repeatedly attacked within the Bible itself. The first thing we notice when reading about God in the Bible is that we are confronted, not with a poverty of descriptions concerning God, but rather with an excess of them. We do not find some simple, linear understanding of YHWH developing through the text, and thus we do not find a single, coherent definition of God, as proclaimed by many contemporary churches. In the Bible we find a vast array of competing stories concerning the character of God that are closely connected to the concrete circumstances of those who inhabit the narrative. Just as personality tests offer us an unrealistic image of ourselves as a single whole, overlooking the fact that we are not only many different things in many different situations but also changing over time, so Western theology has all too often reduced the beautifully varied and complex descriptions of God found in the Bible to a singular reading that does violence to its vibrant nature. The Bible

12

itself is a dynamic text full of poetry, prose, history, law and myth all clashing together in a cacophony of voices. We are presented with a warrior God and a peacemaker, a God of territorial allegiance and a God who transcends all territorial divides, an unchanging God and a God who can be redirected, a God of peace and a God of war, a God who is always watching the world and a God who fails to notice the oppression against Israel in Egypt.[8]

The interesting thing about all this is not that these conflicts exist but that we know they exist. In other words, the writers and editors of the text did not see any reason to try and iron out these inconsistencies – inconsistencies that make any systematic attempt to master the text both violent and irredeemably impossible. Unlike the modern ideal of systematization in definition, these people celebrated the fact that, as Meister Eckhart once claimed, the unnameable is omni-nameable. Evidently such conflicts were not judged to be problematic but were accepted. Indeed, such fissures help to prevent us from forming an idol-atrous image of God, ensuring that none of us can legitimately claim to understand God as God really is. Consequently the text bars any attempt at colonization by individuals or groups who claim to possess an insight into its true meaning. The biblical text resists such idolatrous readings precisely because it contains so many ideological voices, held together in creative tension, ensuring the impossibility of any final resolution. The result is not an account that is hopelessly ideological, but rather a text that shows the extent to which no one ideology or group of ideologies can lay hold of the divine. The text is not only full of fractures, tensions and contradictions but informs us that fractures, tensions and contradictions are all we can hope for.

Yet the Bible not only describes God with a multitude of names; there are also key moments when we find that this is complemented by the idea of God standing beyond every name. We can see this at work in one of the most well-known examples of idolatry in the Bible, namely when the Israelites forge a golden calf after Moses goes to commune with God for 40 days and 40 nights. While Moses is absent the Israelites become anxious and approach Aaron with the following demand: 'Come, make us gods who will go before us. As for this fellow Moses who brought us up out of Egypt, we don't know what has happened to him.'[9] The story goes that Aaron then asked the people to take their golden earrings and bring them before him so that a statue of a calf could be cast. Before this statue many of the people proclaimed: 'These are your gods, O Israel, who brought you out of Egypt.'[10]

This story has often been understood as a defiant and rebellious turning away from God. Yet the text itself tells us that the calf was not originally meant as an alternative to, or reification of, God but was designed as a visual aid to worship. After all, Aaron attempts to point out the limitations of the calf by proclaiming a day of festival specifically in the name of YHWH.[11] The point was that it was only meant to be an object that provided a focal point for reflecting upon the genuine experience of God in their midst. Yet the people were quick to view this object as a visual manifestation of the God who delivered them from Egypt. As such the image became an idol to the people and eclipsed the genuine experience of God.

In addition to this, the Old Testament contains numerous warnings about placing the divine into representational form, making clear that God cannot be revealed through human *logos*. For instance, the word *choshek*, used at the beginning of Genesis, describes the darkness that brooded over the surface of the earth, and is also employed to describe the impenetrable veil that shields us from YHWH's unmediated presence, while words such as *'araphel* (darkness) and *'anan* (cloud) are used when referring to the 'appearance' of the divine. We can also note this approach in Exodus when we read that 'the people remained at a distance while Moses approached the thick darkness [*'araphel*] where God was'.[12] We also find similar motifs in Isaiah who uses the word *carthar* to refer to an intentional hiddenness of the divine presence, a word which conjures up notions such as 'absence', 'concealment', 'hiding' and 'keeping secret'.[13]

While this distance is often described as a divine response to people's sins,[14] especially the Israelites' tendency towards idolatry,[15] it is not simply brought on by the transgressions of the people. In addition to this, the term 'holiness' has strong connotations of a God who is beyond all finding out. This is most evident in one of the encounters between Moses and God described in Exodus, in which Moses is protected from God's full presence by nestling in the cleft of a rock. He is thus protected from the death that would result if he were to catch sight of the face of God.[16] A similar biblical motif is also found in Gideon's and Manoah's fear of death before the angel of YHWH,[17] and when Elijah covers his face with a mantle before approaching the mouth of the cave where YHWH stood.[18] In fact, at one point the text informs us that even the mighty seraphim cover their eyes from the presence of the divine,[19] while the Deuteronomic-prophetic tradition regularly refers to the need to destroy any images of God.[20]

The multitude of competing ideological descriptions concerning God, combined with the anti-idolatrous claims of the text, infer that we can only speak of God's otherness and distance even at the very site of revelation. For instance, while we read in Psalm 97.2 that 'cloud and thick darkness are found about him', the cloud and darkness are the very place in which the divine presence is revealed.[21] The image of a cloud is even used as a description of YHWH's chariot.[22]

Indeed, the book of Job can be seen as one of the earliest attempts to critique ideology by describing a God who is not explicable.[23] In response to Job's suffering, his 'comforters' each attempt to provide a theoretical account that would render the situation intelligible. These accounts ultimately fail, not simply because they fail to provide an adequate explanation, but because the situation transcends the possibility of any adequate explanation. On a more fundamental level, the fact that God's name is unpronounceable acts as a symbol of God's otherness. The very fact that the term 'YHWH' lacks the vowels needed for pronunciation reminds us that this 'proper name' is very improper insomuch as it is impossible to say. Unlike the other references to Israel's God, which are either generic terms or descriptions of attributes which the Israelites ascribed to God, the term 'YHWH' preserves the mystery of God.

Such thinking is not restricted to the Old Testament, for in the New Testament we find repeated warnings against the 'lusts of the eyes', which glory in the visible.[24] This is backed up with reflections upon YHWH's invisible nature,[25] inaccessibility,[26] inexpressibility[27] and unsearchable nature.[28] In fact, the apostle Paul can be seen as a strong precursor to the great masters of suspicion, for his recognition of the gulf that exists between God's transcendence and human frailty offers a profound critique of human thinking. Indeed, this can be seen when Paul writes to the Colossians, 'See to it that no one takes you captive through hollow and deceptive philosophy, which depends on human tradition and the basic principles of this world rather than on Christ.'[29]

Here Paul warns us to beware of human abstractions, which can so easily draw us into a conceptual prison. Indeed, it is precisely this idolatry that is denied by John when he writes that 'you have never heard his voice nor seen his form [*eidos*]'[30] and denied by Paul when he writes that Christians 'walk by faith not by sight [*eidos*]'.[31] It is clear that John and Paul are not asserting that no encounter with God is possible, but rather that any encounter with the divine cannot be reduced to an idolatrous understanding.

Revelation as concealment

Far from abolishing the possibility of faith, the critique of ideology in philosophy and the condemnation of idolatry in scripture only undermine a fundamentalist Christianity that would require religious certainty and lay claim to a correct interpretation of God. In contrast, such critiques bring out the fact that revelation, far from being the opposite of concealment, has concealment built into its very heart. For instance, let us imagine entering a museum and contemplating one of the exhibits. The painting could be said to offer us a type of revelation, for it stands before us and communicates a message. However, the message of a piece of art is not simple, singular or able to be mastered. This is evidenced in the fact that different people will take away different meanings from the same artefact, demonstrating that the message is concealed, elusive and fluid. When we ask ourselves about the meaning of the artwork, we are immediately involved in an act of interpretation which is influenced by what we bring to the painting. In a similar way, the revelation of God should be compared to a parable that speaks out of an excess of meaning. This means that revelation offers a wealth of meaning that will be able to speak in different ways to those with ears to hear. The parable is given to us, but at the same time its full wealth of meaning will never be fully mined. It is not reducible to some clear, singular, scientific formula but rather gives rise to a multitude of commentaries. In opposition to this, many Christian communities view the stories and parables of the Bible as raw material to be translated into a single, understandable meaning rather than experienced as infinitely rich treasures that can speak to us in a plurality of ways.

Hence revelation ought not to be thought of either as that which makes God known or as that which leaves God unknown, but rather as the overpowering light that renders God known *as* unknown. This is not dissimilar to a baby being held by her mother – the baby does not understand the mother but rather experiences being known by the mother. In contrast, revelation is often treated as if it can be deciphered into a dogmatic system rather than embraced as the site where the impenetrable secret of God transforms us. In the former, revelation is rendered into an eloquent doctrine, while in the latter, revelation is that which transforms. We are like an infant in the arms of God, unable to grasp but being transformed by the grasp. Revelation can thus be described as bringing to light the secret of God in such a way that it remains secret. God is thus the secret who remains concealed in the sharing. We can thus not speak of a hidden side of God and a manifest side, for we must acknowledge that the manifest side of God is also hidden.

What is important about revelation is not that we seek to interpret it in the same way but rather that we all love it and are transformed by it. To fail to recognize this would be similar to an art critic saying that what is important when considering a piece of art is that we interpret it correctly rather than loving it and being challenged by it. Indeed, this is what happens when we see various groups and denominations being set up that are founded upon the supposedly 'correct' interpretation of revelation. While joining together in groups that share the same Christian tradition has an important role, the problem arises when we claim that we have the right interpretation while all those who disagree with us are ignorant, deluded or sinfully turning their eye away from the clear light of revelation.

Such enslavement to the idea of revelation as offering a naked insight into God has meant that the development of a robust theology of reconciliation has always proved difficult within much of the contemporary Church (even though it has often striven to find unity) because of its emphasis upon the primacy of what we believe about our beloved over and above the insight that what unifies us is our desire to embrace the beloved. Instead of finding unity in our position as infants basking in a shared love of the same revelation, we are splintered by the emphasis we illegitimately place upon our interpretation of the revelation. Just as a painting we love will speak to us in different ways at different times (hence the need to return to the art that we love rather than being satisfied by seeing it once), so the revelation of God will speak in multiple ways depending upon the context within which we read it and into which it speaks. In contrast to the emphasis upon the *content* of revelation, those involved in the emerging conversation have understood that we must turn things back onto their feet and find unity in the *event* of revelation.

In short, the emerging conversation is in a unique place to acknowledge the long-forgotten insight that God hides in God's visibility, realizing that revelation embraces concealment at one and the same time as it embraces manifestation and that our various interpretations of revelation will always be provisional, fragile and fragmentary. While all of the Church has maintained that there is a revealed and hidden side of God, the difference here is that we are rediscovering the Barthian insight that even the revealed side of God is mysterious. The emerging Church is thus able to leave aside the need for clarity and open up the way for us to accept the fact that what is important is that we are embraced by the beloved rather than finding agreement concerning how we ought to understand this beloved (as if a baby can only really love her mother if she understands her).

Beyond 'God'

This approach involves an important re-articulation of the relation between our *understanding of God* and *God as God really is*. The primary problem with idolatry is not that it falsely claims to have a connection with God but rather that it falsely claims to understand the God that it is connected to. Yet this does not mean that our definitions of God are somehow unimportant – indeed, they remain vital – it is only that we must recognize the extent to which these reflections fall short of that which they attempt to define and always reflect something of the one who makes the claims. If we fail to recognize that the term 'God' always falls short of that towards which the word is supposed to point, we will end up bowing down before our own conceptual creations forged from the raw materials of our self-image, rather than bowing before the one who stands over and above that creation. Hence Meister Eckhart famously prays, 'God rid me of God',[32] a prayer that acknowledges how the God we are in relationship with is bigger, better and different than our understanding of that God.

Chapter 2

The aftermath of theology

Theology and the voice of God

There is an old anecdote in which a mystic, an evangelical pastor and a fundamentalist preacher die on the same day and awake to find themselves by the pearly gates. Upon reaching the gates they are promptly greeted by Peter, who informs them that before entering heaven they must be interviewed by Jesus concerning the state of their doctrine. The first to be called forward is the mystic, who is quietly ushered into a room. Five hours later the mystic reappears with a smile, saying, 'I thought I had got it all wrong.' Then Peter signals to the evangelical pastor, who stands up and enters the room. After a full day has passed the pastor reappears with a frown and says to himself, 'How could I have been so foolish!' Finally Peter asks the fundamentalist to follow him. The fundamentalist picks up his well-worn Bible and walks into the room. A few days pass with no sign of the preacher, then finally the door swings open and Jesus himself appears, exclaiming, 'How could I have got it all so wrong!'

What is at issue in this anecdote is two different ways of approaching our religious traditions. The first is represented by the Christian mystic who is committed to his tradition yet acknowledges that it falls short of grasping the mind of God. This approach does not deny the existence of a relationship and does not imply that we cannot commit actively to the wisdom of our particular Christian tradition; it simply acknowledges that the relationship we have with God cannot be reduced to our understanding of that relationship. The second way (shown in a weak sense by the evangelical pastor and in a strong sense by the fundamentalist preacher) relates to a type of idolatrous relation in which we believe that our ideas actually represent the way that God and the world really operate. The weak sense, testified to by the pastor, is unintentional and dissipates in the face of divine encounter, while the second, evidenced by the fundamentalist, is Pharisaic in nature, for it refuses to give up its interpretation of God, even in the presence of God. Indeed, this can be seen as one of the central problems with the Pharisees as represented in the New Testament, for they held so closely to their interpretation of the Messiah that when the Messiah finally appeared in a form that was different to what they expected, they rejected the Messiah in order to retain the integrity of their interpretation.

The difference between the idea that our Christian traditions describe God and the view that they are worshipful responses to God is important to grasp, for while the former seeks to define, the latter is engaged with response. By charting the latter course, those within the emerging conversation perceive a very different way of understanding theology. It is no longer thought of as a human discourse that speaks of God but rather as the place where God speaks into human discourse. In other words, theology is understood as the site in which revelation makes its appearance in the world, the place in which *theos* (God) impacts, and overwhelms, the human realm of *logos* (reason). Consequently we do not *do* theology but are rather overcome and transformed by it: we do not master it but are mastered by it.

If theology comes to be understood as the place where God speaks, then we must seek, not to speak of God, but rather to be that place where God speaks. Through our words and actions we seek to be the site of revelation through which people encounter the life-giving Word of God. For some, this change in the understanding of theology seems to undermine the legitimacy of various Christian traditions, and ultimately that of Christianity itself. However, this is not the case. While our religious traditions may not define God, they can be seen to arise in the aftermath of God, both as a means of provisionally understanding what has occurred in the life of the person or community that has been impacted, and as a response to God. Our 'theological' musings can thus be called a/theological insomuch as they acknowledge that we must still speak of God (theology, as traditionally understood) while also recognizing that this speech fails to define God (a/theology).

22

Rather than viewing our traditions as windows through which we can see our beloved, those involved in the emerging conversation acknowledge that our reflections upon God arise as a result of the one who overflows and blinds our understanding. In this way the reflections of our various denominations do not testify directly of God, via their content, but rather testify to God indirectly, via their very existence. The result is not a change in what we think but rather a change in how we think.

God as subject, not object

One way of understanding the relation between God and humanity is through the distinction between knowledge of something as an object and knowledge of something as a subject. To understand this better we may take the example of prisoners in a concentration camp during the Second World War. In these camps the guards treated their prisoners as mere objects. They possessed a vast amount of data concerning such things as their prisoners' age, previous occupation, family background and siblings. Yet this type of knowledge, however comprehensive, is poverty-stricken when compared to the type of knowledge that the prisoners' loved ones would have possessed. While some of the guards may have held more objective data about an individual than that individual's own family, the family would still possess a knowledge of the individual which the soldiers could never gain, a knowledge that is only opened up in love. For while those who imprison us, employ us or sell products to us may treat us as objects, the ones who love us treat us as subjects, subjects who can never be fully grasped in terms of cold facts and statistical probabilities. Indeed this is the difference between love and lust, for while lust treats the other solely as an object to be devoured, love treats the other as a subject who cannot be reduced wholly to an object.

God can never be and ought never to be reduced to a mere object for consideration, for in faith God is experienced as the ultimate subject. God is not a theoretical problem to somehow resolve but rather a mystery to be participated in. This perspective is evidenced in the Bible itself when we note that the term 'knowing' in the Hebrew tradition (in contrast to the Greek tradition) is about engaging in an intimate encounter rather than describing some objective fact: religious truth is thus that which transforms reality rather than that which describes it.

While descriptions concerning the experience of this ineffable encounter differ, there is a certain family resemblance between some of the most sophisticated and sustained attempts at explanation. These include the feeling of absolute dependence (Schleiermacher), the feeling of utter confidence in the face of anything (Barth and Bultmann), the feeling of ultimate concern (Tillich) and the feeling of being preceded by something other (Rosenzweig).[33] Each of these expressions helps to articulate the sense that one is no longer master over one's own existence – that God is not the *object* of our thought but rather the *absolute subject* before whom *we are the object*. This is confirmed in baptism when we say that we are 'baptized into the name of the Father, Son and Holy Ghost'. Here we do not name God but God's name names us.

God as hyper-present

By offering a robust a/theology which acknowledges the proper place of doubt, ambiguity, complexity and mystery, we acknowledge that God's interaction with the world is irreducible to understanding, precisely because God's presence is a type of hyper-presence. Hyper-presence is a term that refers to a type of divine saturation that exists in the heart of God's presence. It means that God not only overflows and overwhelms our understanding but also overflows and overwhelms our experience. While many of the communities taking part in the emerging conversation engage in highly creative forms of religious activity, encouraging a full range of sensual experience in worship, it would be a mistake to think that such openness to other languages (such as those of painting, poetry and ritual) allows privileged access to God that is inaccessible to reason. While helping to reintroduce a wide range of experience to worship, those involved in the emerging conversation testify to the idea that God can no more be contained in experience than in language. While both expressions are impor-tant, they each testify to that which cannot be contained in either. Indeed, one of the reasons why many of the communities involved in the emerging conversation engage in creative forms of worship lies, not in the conviction that opening up a wider array of sense experience in worship will lead to a more effective grasping of God, but rather in the fact that, in the aftermath of God, all our being cries out in response.

The acknowledgement that God is hyper-present has inspired Christians throughout history to think up different ways to express God as revealed through Christ. For instance, Paul Tillich spoke of the 'God beyond God'; Jean-Luc Marion writes the word 'God' with a St Andrew's cross through the centre; and Meister Eckhart spoke of forsaking God for the sake of God.

The un/known God

What is beginning to arise from the discussion so far is the idea that God ought to be understood as radically transcendent, not because God is somehow distant and remote from us, but precisely because God is immanent. In the same way that the sun blinds the one who looks directly at its light, so God's incoming blinds our intellect. In this way the God who is testified to in the Judeo-Christian tradition saturates our understanding with a blinding presence. This type of transcendent-immanence can be described as 'hypernymity'. While anonymity offers too little information for our understanding to grasp (like a figure on television who has been veiled in darkness so as to protect their identity), hypernymity gives us far too much information. Instead of being limited by the poverty of absence we are short-circuited by the excess of presence. The anonymous and the hypernymous both resist reduction to complete understanding, but for very different reasons.

It is unfortunate that this radical understanding of transcendence has largely been lost in the contemporary Church and is generally thought to be the polar opposite of immanence. The result of such thinking is the development of a false dichotomy that allows for disagreement between those churches which are accused of maintaining the idea of a distant God and those which are critiqued for celebrating immanence at the expense of God's holiness. Yet in reality the Christian God destroys the idea of immanence and transcendence

25

as opposite points in a diffuse spectrum, replacing this with the idea that immanence and transcendence are one and the same point: God remains transcendent amidst immanence precisely because God remains concealed amidst revelation. In this reading, Christ, as the image of the invisible God, both reveals and conceals God: rendering God known while simultaneously maintaining divine mystery. Here the God testified to in Christianity is affirmed as an un/known God.

Christianity as a/theistic

This recognition of hyper-presence leads us to reconsider the traditional atheism/theism opposition, for if our beliefs necessarily fall short of that which they attempt to describe, then it would seem that a certain atheistic spirit is actually deeply embedded within Christianity. The term 'atheism' can be understood in a number of ways. For instance, it can refer to the belief that the universe is all there is (existing without source or as its own source), or to the idea that the term 'God' is meaningless, incoherent or irrelevant (although this could more accurately be called 'anti-theism'), or to the disbelief in some particular god or cluster of gods. The latter use of the word has always been acknowledged as part of Christianity; indeed, the early Christians were called atheists because their own affirmation of God involved a rejection of the gods advocated by the Roman Empire. Yet the atheistic spirit within Christianity delves much deeper than this – for we disbelieve not only in other gods but also in the God that we believe in.

As we have seen, we ought to affirm our view of God while at the same time realizing that that view is inadequate. Hence we act both as theist and atheist. This a/theism is not some agnostic middle point hovering hesitantly between theism and atheism but, rather, actively embraces both out of a profound faith. Just as Christianity does not rest between transcendence and immanence but holds both extremes simultaneously, so too it holds atheism and theism together in the cradle of faith.

This a/theistic approach is deeply deconstructive since it always prevents our ideas from scaling the throne of God. Yet it is important to bear in mind that this deconstruction is not destruction, for the questioning it engages in is not designed to undermine God but to affirm God. This method is similar to that practised by the original cynics who, far from being nihilists and relativists, were deeply moral individuals who questioned the ethical conduct they saw around them precisely because they loved morality so much. This a/theism is thus a deeply religious and faith-filled form of cynical discourse, one which captures how faith operates in an oscillation between understanding and unknowing. This unknowing is to be utterly distinguished from an intellectually lazy ignorance, for it is a type of unknowing which arises not from imprecision but rather from deep reflection and sustained meditation.

The a/theistic language employed by those involved in the emerging conversation is not merely a way of shedding some inaccurate ideas we have picked up about God and faith before we can begin the serious task of construction, and it is certainly not a provisional clearing away that must happen before a new religious structure is built: rather it is a recognition that negation is embedded within, and permeates, all religious affirmation. It is an acknowledgement that a desert of ignorance exists in the midst of every oasis of understanding.

This means that the emerging thought is a self-acknowledged form of heresy insomuch as it is aware of its failure to describe that of which it speaks. This recognition acts as an effective theological response to fundamentalism, as it unsettles the dark heart of its self-certain power. Very briefly, fundamentalism can be understood as a particular way of believing one's beliefs rather than referring to the actual content of one's beliefs. It can be described as holding a belief system in such a way that it mutually excludes all other systems, rejecting other views in direct proportion to how much they differ from one's own. In contrast, the a/theistic approach can be seen as a form of disbelieving what one believes, or rather, believing *in* God while remaining dubious concerning what one believes *about* God (a distinction that fundamentalism is unable to maintain). This does not actually contradict the idea of orthodoxy but rather allows us to understand it in a new light (which is the subject of the next chapter).

The point is not that our beliefs are inherently problematic but only that they become problematic when held in a manner that would claim more than some provisional, pragmatic response to

27

that which transcends conceptualization. This a/theistic approach is not to be mistaken for some type of synthesis of opposites; rather, it is the uncollapsible tension between affirming our religious ideas while also placing them into question. This a/theism is not then some temporary place of uncertainty on the way to spiritual maturity, but rather is something that operates within faith as a type of heat-inducing friction that prevents our liquid images of the divine from cooling and solidifying into idolatrous form.

This approach reflects the writings of such Christian thinkers as Justin Martyr, St Pantaenus, Clement of Alexandria and Origen, who, although affirming the divine presence, wrote insightfully about the danger of reducing God to a reflection of human rationality and counselled their readers about the need to prostrate the intellect before God. For instance, Gregory of Nyssa speaks of the move towards God as a journey into divine darkness, arguing that while religious knowledge begins as an experience of entering into the light, the deeper we go, the more darkness we find in that light.[34] Or as the fifth-century mystic St Leo the Great wrote:

> Even if one has progressed far in divine things, one is never nearer the truth than when one understands that those things still remain to be discovered. He who believes he has attained the goal, far from finding what he seeks, falls by the wayside.[35]

This is a realization borne from a hermeneutic approach that is profoundly sensitive to human finitude.

Augustine also delves into this tradition, encouraging us to bear in mind that God transcends all terms and escapes every conceptualization – even that of being beyond conceptualization.[36] Yet one of the most influential thinkers of this tradition was Pseudo-Dionysius, whose *Mystical Theology* is a razor-sharp attack upon speculative thought and stresses the need for liberation from the idolatry of abstraction. Thinking along the same lines as Augustine, though expressing the matter more explicitly, Pseudo-Dionysius articulates an understanding of the divine as beyond the reach of all thinking, whether affirmation or negation:

> While he possesses all the positive attributes of the universe (being the universal Cause) yet, in a more strict sense, He does not possess them,

since He transcends them all; wherefore there is no contradiction between the affirmations and the negations, insomuch as He infinitely precedes all conceptions of deprivation, being beyond all positive and negative distinctions.[37]

Here we witness a way of thinking that seeks to go beyond saying both what God is and what God is not. Union with the divine, on this reading, involves a knowing unknowing in which the individual is radically undone. With this in mind, he writes:

Leave behind the senses and the operations of the intellect, and all things sensible and intellectual, and all things in the world of being and non-being, that thou mayest arise by unknowing towards the union, as far as it is attainable, with him who transcends all being and all knowledge.[38]

Pseudo-Dionysius argues that this knowing unknowing acknowledges its profound finitude and inability to grasp that to which the religious individual intends. This divine darkness represents a type of supra-darkness that stands in sharp contradistinction to the sub-darkness of a desolate nihilism. While one is brought about by an absolute excess of light, the other results from a total absence; while one represents a higher form of unknowing that subverts reasoning, the other signals mere ignorance.

Indeed, Anselm, who is often seen as a key thinker in claiming that God is conceivable, writes that when gazing upon the Lord, the eye is darkened, noting that:

Surely it is both darkened in itself and dazzled by you. Indeed it is both obscured by its own littleness and overwhelmed by your vastness.[39]

Indeed, in chapter 15 of the *Proslogion* we find the following (non)definition of God:

Therefore, Lord, you are not merely that than which a greater cannot be thought; you are something greater than can be thought. For since it is possible to think that such a being exists, then if you are not that being, it is possible to think something greater than you. But that is impossible.[40]

This hypernymity is reflected in the thought of Simeon the New Theologian when he encourages his readers to:

Think of a man standing at night inside his house, with all the doors closed; and then suppose that he opens a window just at the moment when there is a sudden flash of lightning. Unable to bear its brightness, at once he protects himself by closing his eyes and drawing back from the window. So it is with the soul that is enclosed in the realm of the senses; if ever she peeps out through the window of the intellect, she is overwhelmed by the brightness, the lightning, of the pledge of the Holy Spirit that is within her. Unable to bear the splendour of the unveiled light, at once she is bewildered in her intellect, and draws back entirely upon herself, taking refuge, as in a house, among sensory and human beings.[41]

By recognizing the limits of human finitude Anselm formulates a definition of God that respects the transcendence of God. Hence his repeated reference to the Bible verse that declares, 'God dwells in inaccessible light'.[42] This reading of Anselm has been largely overlooked because his claim that God is 'something than which nothing greater can be thought'[43] is interpreted as a definition of God rather than a (non)definition. Indeed, it has the form of a definition but actually ascribes no positive essence to the divine: it does not say that God is the greatest conceivable being but rather that a greater than God cannot be thought. We can indeed conceive of something beyond thought but we cannot think of something beyond that.

For Anselm, the concept 'God' must include the idea of how the object of the concept transcends every concept. As the contemporary philosopher Jean-Luc Marion writes, 'The root of the argument is not reliance on the concept but reliance on a non-concept, acknowledged as such.'[44] This was something hinted at by the nineteenth-century Russian 'hole worshippers' who drilled holes in their walls and then prayed to them. Here the void that is prayed to replaces any divine object with empty space.[45]

For Anselm there are three levels of existence. The first, and lowest, level is that which exists only in the mind (for instance, a unicorn). The second refers to those things that exist both in the mind and in reality (such as a horse). The third level is that which exists in reality but which cannot be contained in the mind (i.e. God). It is this third level of existence that has often been overlooked by the Church, and yet it is here that we find God.

By exploring the idea that God cannot be reduced to our under-standing or experience, we can already draw out two insights regarding the a/theological approach. First, this a/theology views our denominations as arising as a response to God; and second, it acknowledges that these denominations do not make objective claims concerning God. In short, it sees our various denominations as different ways of speaking about our beloved in a manner which maintains epistemological silence.[46] We must speak and yet we must maintain our silence, we must maintain distance amidst the proximity of God, and we must worship while being careful not to make God into the object of our worship: for God is the subject before whom we worship. This site of uncertainty and unknowing is often a fright-ening place to dwell, but while the comfort provided by religion is placed into a certain distress by the idea of doubt, this distress, too, is not without a certain comfort. For while we do not grasp God, faith is born amidst the feeling that God grasps us.

Chapter 3

A/theology as icon

—◆—

Dis-courses

So far we have explored the idea that, by employing the concept of hypernymity, those involved in the emerging conversation are in a unique position to find a way beyond the naïve view that we can speak of God and the defeatist notion that we must give up on God. By combining theism and atheism in an a/theistic discourse we are able to develop a way of thinking that brings the speaker into an awareness of his or her limitations and a space of knowledgeable ignorance. Here the religious participant is addressed, transformed and grasped by that which they cannot contain: they feel themselves to be the subject of an object that cannot be objectified.

It is precisely this approach that allows those involved in the emerging conversation to form an a/theological way of speaking that maintains denominational differences while crossing denominational barriers. This emerging a/theology can thus be described as a genuinely ecumenical device, for by unsettling and decentring any idea of a one, true interpretation held by one group over and against all the others, a network of bridges is formed between different interpretative communities who acknowledge that we are all engaged in an interpretive process which can never do justice to the revelation itself.[47] The approach itself can no more be described as a liberal perspective than it can be viewed as conservative. Indeed it challenges all, whether conservative or liberal, to acknowledge the limits of these views. As the psychologist Victor Frankl once pointed out, true knowledge is always *knowledge plus* – that is, knowledge that understands that it is always penetrated by unknowing. The result is that God is not defined as the greatest conceivable being or as that which is greater than conception, but rather, as Anselm argued, God is the *one who is conceived as inconceivable.* In other words, it is precisely God's participation with us that allows us to understand that God is beyond understanding.

Returning again to the analogy of a painting, those in the emerging conversation understand that what unites Christians is not that we somehow grasp the true meaning (another way of saying 'my meaning') of the painting, as if it can be reduced to a singular message, but that we are seduced and transformed by it. Those within the emerging conversation find unity not by a type of cloning by which all Christians are encouraged to believe the same thing, thus forming one master denomination, but amidst denominational diversity.

The deconstructive language being forged here acknowledges itself as a *dis-course* that sends us *off-course* – that is, our reflections on God never bring us to God. If we imagine that our words are like arrows, then we can say that those arrows always fall short of the heavenly realm to which we aim them. In short, an emerging discourse acknowledges that *speaking of God is never speaking of God but only ever speaking about our understanding of God.* What we think and say about God is still both important and unavoidable, for our words help us come to terms with the hallowed mystery and respond to it. However, this approach diligently maintains a conceptual distance between ourselves and God, one which approaches the divine mystery as something to be transformed by rather than solved.

This a/theology does not deny the existence of revelation but rather affirms the central idea of Chapter 1, namely that revelation is in no way opposed to concealment, but rather has concealment built into its very heart. In order to express this approach, we must engage in a type of fractured discourse as evidenced by Jesus in the opening words of the Lord's Prayer. Here we read that Jesus taught his disciples to pray by beginning with the words: 'Our Father in heaven, hallowed be your name.' Here God is named 'Father', yet immediately the prayer acknowledges that this name is 'hallowed'. We are thus informed that the name is holy and set apart, operating in a way that is other than we imagine, transcending all earthly names and escaping our attempts at definition.[48] God is simultaneously both named and unnamed, reminding us that our understanding of fatherhood is profoundly affected by our cultural embeddedness. This becomes clear as we consider how the idea of fatherhood differs between cultures existing at the same time and within cultures at different times. Indeed, even the most fundamental statements, such as 'God is love', need to be deconstructed in this way, for while we can all agree that believers affirm the central idea that God is love, if we were to ask a dozen Christians from around the world to write an essay on what this means, there would be a wide diversity of thought. While we may say that God is love, we must acknowledge that God is also hallowed, and thus my understanding of love will be inadequate.

Doubt as virtue

Yet an objection can be raised that this perspective fundamentally undermines the Christian faith, for if God cannot be adequately grasped, then how can we know for sure that what is grasping us is God? It is argued that if the emerging community follows this line of thinking, then it will ultimately find itself hacking away at the tree under which it shelters, for surely everything is radically undermined by the uncertainty that ensues from the idea of God as hypernonymous.

The problem with this objection is not that its main insight concerning the introduction of doubt is incorrect but rather that it fundamentally misunderstands the role of that doubt within religion. In contrast to the modern view that religious doubt is something to reject, fear or merely tolerate, doubt not only can be seen as an inevitable aspect of our humanity but also can be celebrated as a vital part of faith. Doubt has often been disparaged, or merely tolerated, because it is seen as leading to an inert state of undecidability in which nothing can be believed or acted upon. Yet in reality it is only in the midst of undecidability that real decisions can be made.

For instance, take the example of two people getting married with the firm conviction that the union will last as long as they both live. In this state of obvious delusion no real decision needs to be made. The future is believed to be so certain that the decision to marry requires no decision at all. Yet if two people understand that their relationship will face various hardships, that the future is uncertain and that there are no guarantees, then, far from preventing a decision, this is the very point when a real decision needs to be made. The vows of marriage are not so much affirmations of what one believes will take place but rather promises that one will work towards ensuring that it will indeed happen. To decide for marriage knowing that all manner of things may conspire against the union is to make a truly daring and authentic decision – the only type of decision worthy of the name. Here we can see that doubt provides the context out of which real decision occurs and real love is tested, for love will say 'yes' regardless of uncertainty. A love that requires contracts and absolute assurance in order to act is no love at all.

In the same way, the believer who encounters serious doubt does not renounce his or her faith but rather uses it as an opportunity to affirm it. We may call this acknowledgement of doubt a Holy Saturday experience (a term that refers to the 24 hours nestled between the crucifixion and resurrection of Christ). This day marked a moment of great uncertainty and darkness for the followers of Jesus. Yet it is precisely in the midst of a Holy Saturday experience that the decision to follow Christ becomes truly authentic. A faith that can only exist in the light of victory and certainty is one which really affirms the self while pretending to affirm Christ, for it only follows Jesus in the belief that Jesus has conquered death. Yet a faith that can look at the horror of the cross and still say 'yes' is one that says 'no' to the self in saying 'yes' to Christ. If one loses one's life only because one believes that this is the way to find it, then one gives up nothing; to truly lose one's life, one must lay down that life without regard to whether or not one finds it. Only a genuine faith can embrace doubt, for such a faith does not act because of a self-interested reason (such as fear of hell or desire for heaven) but acts simply because it must. A real follower of Jesus would commit to him before the crucifixion, between the crucifixion and the resurrection, and after the resurrection.

This is in no way equivalent to saying that the Christian ought to adopt a position of disinterested agnosticism – far from it. The point is only that the believer should not repress the shadow of doubt that hangs over all belief (the potential *lie* that may dwell in the heart of every be*lief*). Instead the believer ought to acknowledge and even celebrate this dark night of the soul, understanding that this is not a threatening darkness which conceals an enemy but rather is the intimate darkness within which we embrace our faith. For when we can say that we will follow God regardless of the uncertainty involved in such a decision, then real faith is born – for love acts not whenever a certain set of criteria has been met, but rather because it is in the nature of love to act.

The end of apologetics

The fear and rejection of doubt as a legitimate part of faith can be seen at its most stark in the twentieth-century Church's obsession with the area of apologetics (a term which refers to a formal justification or defence of doctrine). Legal terminology is often employed within this apologetic discourse so as to give the impression that Christianity can be proven beyond all reasonable doubt by a cold and objective analysis of the empirical evidence for its claims. Broadly speaking, we can identify two types of apologetic procedure employed by the Church: word and wonder. The first of these builds an apologetic case via the use of reason so as to logically convince the other that Christianity is compelling and must be accepted by anyone who wishes to be rational. The second builds an apologetic case via the use of the miraculous in order to demonstrate to the other that they ought to believe. Because of their compelling nature, these apologetic strategies can be termed 'power discourses'. Yet it is precisely against these power discourses that the emerging community must take its stand, offering instead a genuinely Christlike and effective alternative.

These power discourses of word and wonder attempt to present faith in such a way that rejection, if not impossible, is utterly irrational. In this way, the acceptance or rejection of the system is based, not upon a love for the system or a feeling of overwhelming seduction by it, but rather upon the accumulation of evidence that stands secure, regardless of the motive and desires of the individual. In short, power discourses operate at the level of command. For instance, if someone is convinced that there is a place where they will be tormented after death, and that the only way to avoid this terror is by affirming that

Jesus Christ is Lord, then they will no doubt make that affirmation, regardless of whether they are genuinely moved by Christ or not. This type of discourse endeavours to compel individuals to bow their knee regardless of their motives or the nature of their desire. Like a lover of nuts who is offered thousands of shells with no centre, so we offer God thousands of 'converts' with no heart. In opposition to this, the apostle Paul introduces a different kind of discourse altogether:

> When I came to you, brothers, I did not come with eloquence or super-ior wisdom as I proclaimed to you the testimony about God. For I resolved to know nothing while I was with you except Jesus Christ and him crucified. I came to you in weakness and fear, and much trembling. My message and my preaching were not with wise and persuasive words, but with a demonstration of the Spirit's power, so that your faith may not rest on men's wisdom, but on God's power.[49]

He constantly refrains from resting his faith on wise words or the miraculous, instead endeavouring to create a space for the 'Spirit's power' to arrive, a power that is not compelled by human might or miraculous wonder. Unlike the traditional mode of preaching, which seeks to persuade and clarify, this discourse maintains the object of communication as obscure and unobjectifiable. Instead of closing thought down – by telling people what they ought to think – this discourse opens up thought. Unlike the discourse of apologetics and the discourse of the miracle (which each attempt to forcibly bring people to their knees), the discourse of Paul acts as an aroma. Following this approach, we can draw out how the believer ought to be seen as the poem, parable and salt of God in the world rather than God's proposition to the world. Indeed, Jesus offers the paradigmatic example of a powerless discourse by saying radically different things to different people, relating in a singular manner to what each indi-vidual requires rather than extrapolating upon some universal abstract system. He gave neither philosophical reflection to those who sought wisdom nor miracles to those who desired a sign. If we are to guess a motive for Jesus' miracles, then we would have to think that he performed them out of love rather than as a means of compelling belief. Indeed, he often asked that people keep the healings a secret (unlike much of the Church today, which would use miraculous signs in a public manner in order to compel people to believe) and did not follow them up with a sinner's prayer. A powerless discourse is not against the use of word or wonder at all, for it is reason that helps us understand the limits of reason and it is the miraculous which can bring the healing of God.

In order to better understand this approach, it is helpful to make a distinction between the ideas of a hint and an order. Take the example of two people in a room. If one has authority over the other and commands the other to close the door, the other will of course close it, regardless of whether or not he or she likes the authority figure, since if an authority figure gives a command, obedience is the sole requirement. Yet, in opposition to this power discourse, the powerless discourse is analogous to one person saying to their equal that they are a little cold. In this way, one speaks in such a way that hints (but does not demand) that they would like the door to be closed. If the other is a caring individual, he or she will be likely to close the door, and if not, he or she will probably ignore what was said. The hint speaks to the heart and will only be heard by those with a sensitive and open ear. This powerless discourse of the hint can be seen at work in Jesus' parables, which can only truly be heard by those 'with ears to hear'. Instead of religious discourse being a type of drink designed to satisfy our thirst for answers, Jesus made his teaching salty, evoking thirst. Instead of offering a scientific explanation that would convince, or publicizing the miracles so as to compel his listeners, Jesus engaged in a poetic discourse that spoke to the heart of those who would listen. In a world where people believe they are not hungry, we must not offer food but rather an aroma that helps them desire the food that we cannot provide. We are a people who are born from a response to hints of the divine. Not only this, but we must embrace the idea that we are also called to be hints of the divine.

Iconic God-talk

Far from this powerless *dis*-course resulting in a relativistic form of religiosity, it provides the path which leads to a more appropriate way of speaking, acting and believing, for once we reject the idolatrous approach to faith, we are left with what can be called an iconic approach.

Unlike idolatry, which claims to make manifest the very essence of God, or the humanistic approach, which claims that God, if God exists, is utterly irrelevant, the iconic approach offers a different way of understanding. To treat something as an icon is to view particular words, images or experiences as aids in contemplation of that which cannot be reduced to words, images or experience. Not only this, but the icon represents a place where God touches humanity. Consequently, icons are not only the place where we contemplate God; they also act as the place that God uses in order to communicate with us.

A helpful way of reflecting upon this involves thinking about how we interact with other people's flesh. We can think of three basic ways that we can look at another. The first can be described as lust and involves reducing somebody to their purely physical appearance. The second could be called indifference and refers to times in which we see a person's flesh and yet pay no attention to it – for instance, walking down a busy street can involve seeing hundreds of people while paying no real attention to any of them. The third way can be described in terms of love. In love we value the flesh of our beloved, but we do not reduce them to their flesh. In particular, the face of our beloved is important, for in his or her facial expressions we are able to perceive the existence of various emotions and feelings that are otherwise unavailable to us. Not only this, but when we look at the face of our beloved we are aware that we are looking at one who looks back at us. We cannot see the gaze of the one who looks but we can sense it; indeed, the experience of being looked at can often be powerful and unnerving. The face of our beloved can thus be described as an icon. Just as with an idol, it is the way we interact with an object, rather than a property in the object itself, that renders it an icon. But in the look of love, objects are exposed as icons. The face of our beloved is not a signpost, for a signpost is not the place where it points; yet neither is the face a pure manifestation of our beloved. Rather, the face is the place where the beloved is both revealed and hidden.

This is beautifully expressed in Sam Mendes' *American Beauty*. At one point in the film Jane Bernhman (Thora Birch) is in her bedroom. Her window happens to overlook her neighbour's house, and after a few moments she notices, from the corner of her eye, that she is being recorded on a camcorder from a room across the drive by her seemingly eccentric neighbour Ricky Fitts (Wes Benthley). Jane slowly approaches the window and begins to strip for the camera. When she has removed her clothes, the camera shot cuts from Jane's bedroom to where Ricky is filming. It is now that we can see what he is recording – her eyes. Here Ricky is portrayed as not merely absorbed by Jane's flesh but rather as one who is seeking transcendence within it, loving it while not being enslaved by it.

A/theology as transformative

This iconic understanding of faith not only allows us to view our religious traditions as an aid to reflection, but they can be held as wisdom narratives that help us to work out how to live as followers of Christ. Our traditions teach us certain spiritual disciplines that have been useful for others in developing their relation with the divine and in their endeavour to become the theological site where God speaks. Yet that does not mean that these spiritual disciplines are magic formulas. Rather, they are more like pragmatic disciplines. The following story may help illuminate this:

> There was once a wise teacher who would go to the temple every evening to pray with his disciples. By the temple there was a stray cat who would wander in every evening during these prayers and disturb the peace. So, each evening before prayers the teacher would tie the cat to a tree outside before entering. The teacher was old and passed away a few years later. His disciples continued to tie the cat to the tree each evening before prayers.
>
> Eventually the cat died and so some of the disciples purchased a new cat so that they could continue the ritual. After a hundred years the tree died and a new one was quickly planted so that the cat (by now the eighth-generation cat) could be tied to it. Over the centuries learned scholars began to write books on the symbolic meaning of the act.

Here we witness how a pragmatic activity used in order to aid worship can easily become a mechanical activity devoid of power. The ways of prayer, fasting, meditation, study, silence and so on have been discovered to aid a relationship with God; however, one person's method of employing these will not be the same as another's. We must not despise the other because their use of these is different to our own, and neither should we feel condemned if our use of them is different from those whom we respect and admire.

The point of this a/theology is that it understands that God is testified to in the transformed lives of believers rather than in some abstract doctrinal system, and that our particular Christian tradition is the means by which our ancestors speak their wisdom in aiding this transformed life. As a result, those involved in the emerging conversation are not forced to choose between the fundamentalist view of those who claim that they know God's thoughts and the humanist idea that the term 'God' is a meaningless nonsense. Far from running from the insights that derive from the critique of ideology, the emerging community can embrace them by developing the idea that while our conceptual constructions always express the individual or community (describe your God and you will discover yourself), they can still be thought of as having been birthed from a genuine encounter and as offering advice on how we should live in a way that facilitates that encounter.

Not only this, but such an iconic approach is concerned with worship and prayer. Instead of saying anything positive or negative regarding God, it provides a way of avoiding idolatrous talk in favour of heartfelt praise. In this iconic understanding, our thoughts concerning God are directed towards God in love rather than enslaving God with words.

The saying of nothing

In contrast to the view that evangelism is that which gives an answer for those who are asking, we must have faith to believe that those who seek will find for themselves (indeed, Chapter 4 will attempt to show that genuine seeking is finding). If this is true, then the job of the Church is not to provide an answer – for the answer is not a phrase or doctrine – but rather to help encourage the religious question to arise. In contrast to the type of sermon that aims to answer thought by providing a clear explanation of a passage or area of Christian life, the emerging community is in a unique place to embrace a type of communication that opens up thought by asking questions and celebrating complexity.

Christianity thus engages in a pragmatic discourse which intends towards the one who lies beyond all language. As such, the language of faith is at its best when it both remembers its profound limitations and simultaneously places us in a clearing within which we can be addressed by God. This offers a type of Copernican revolution in which the individual no longer imposes a *logos* upon the divine but rather is placed under the shadow of the divine *logos*.

The silence that is part of all God-talk is not the silence of banality, indifference or ignorance but one that stands in awe of God. This does not necessitate an absolute 'silencing', whereby we give up speaking of God, but rather involves a recognition that our language concerning the divine remains silent in its speech. As Marion writes, 'The silence suitable to God requires knowing how to remain silent, not out of agnosticism (the polite surname of impossible atheism) or out of humiliation, but simply out of respect.'[50] Or as Gregory Palamas writes, '[The] super-essential nature of God is not a subject for speech or thought or even contemplation, for it is far removed from all that exists . . . [it is] incomprehensible and ineffable to all for ever.'[51]

Central to this approach is the idea that God stands outside our language regimes and cannot be colonized via any power discourse. This means that the Christian faith is extrapolated via a powerless discourse which, at its most evangelical, attempts to create a space in which others can seek for themselves. Consequently, one of the roles of the Church is to provide a sacred space for this exploration. Instead of the evangelist stepping up when someone shows an interest in religious matters, this is precisely the point when they should step down. Consequently, the faithful attempt to create a space where the Christ-event is encouraged to arrive both in themselves and in others. The religious individual tears out all the idolatrous ideas that have impregnated the womb of his or her being, becoming like

Mary, so that the Christ-event can be conceived within him or her – an event whose transformative power is matched only by its impenetrable mystery.

So in a sense, when it comes to God, we have nothing to say to others and we must not be ashamed of saying it. Our approach must be a powerless one which employs words as a way of saying that we have been left utterly breathless by a beauty that surpasses all words. This does not mean that we remain silent – far from it. The desire to get beyond language forces us to stretch language to its very limits. As Samuel Beckett once commented, we use words in order to tear through them and glimpse at what lies beneath. The desire to say nothing, to create sacred space, opens up the most beautiful type of language available – the language of parables, prose and poetry. This is why the mystics would write so extensively about how nothing can be written and would preach beautiful sermons about the futility of words. Without such well-honed words we may begin to think that we have something to say instead of viewing our life as the space out of which God speaks. When we speak into the void, we create life-less idols; when God speaks into the void, the void teems with life.

For those within the emerging conversation this a/theology is not a way of understanding God and neither is it simply the result of filtering God through our minds in order for God to be provisionally understood. Rather, our a/theology should be thought of as a dark glass which protects God from being spoken, which responds to and returns to the love of God, and which encourages others to seek God for themselves. God is not revealed via our words but rather via the life of the transformed individual.

In this way the emerging conversation is demonstrating an ability to stand up and engage in a powerless, space-creating discourse that opens up thinking and offers hints rather than orders. In short, the emerging community must endeavour to be a question rather than an answer and an aroma rather than food. It must seek to offer an approach that enables the people of God to become the parable, aroma and salt of God in the world, helping to form a space where God can give of God. For too long the Church has been seen as an oasis in the desert – offering water to those who are thirsty. In contrast, the emerging community appears more as a desert in the oasis of life, offering silence, space and desolation amidst the sickly nourishment of Western capitalism. It is in this desert, as we wander together as nomads, that God is to be found. For it is here that we are nourished by our hunger.

Chapter 4

Inhabiting the God-shaped hole

———◆◆◆———

Religion and the absence of God

Recently, when I was presenting a paper to the Belfast humanist society, I was asked how I could possibly believe that my own religious tradition was true, given the fact that recent estimates put the number of religions in the world at approximately 4,200. The only answer I could give to this question was, 'I don't.' While I found myself hesitant about speaking of religions that I knew nothing about, I was quite confident in asserting that my own religion was not true. This response was met by the question as to why I would affiliate myself with the Christian religion if I did not believe that it revealed God. Yet far from being a reason to reject Christianity, this is precisely one of the reasons why I embrace it, for in Jesus I see not merely an individual who acted as a catalyst for a new religious movement, but also a subversive prophet who signalled the end of all religious movements. To be part of the Christian religion is to simultaneously hold that religion lightly.

Here I was attempting to draw out how Jesus employed a deeply deconstructive approach to religion which both affirmed and critiqued the movement that began in his lifetime. Christianity, following this deconstructive and subversive element in the life of Jesus, is then a religion which critiques its own religiosity. In order to understand this, it is important to begin with a deeper understanding of the term 'religion'. Etymologically speaking, the word itself evolved from the eleventh-century Anglo-French term *religiun*, a word that connotes a way of life structured by monastic vows and indicates the belief in a divine power. This word can itself be seen to spring from two possible sources. First, it can be seen to derive from the Latin root *religio*, meaning a respect and reverence for the gods; this word has connections with the term *relegare*, referring to a type of re-reading or return (from *re*, meaning 'again', and *legere*, meaning 'read'). Second, there is the popular connection of the term with *religare*, which means to bind fast (from which we get the word 'rely') via an obligation that connects humans and gods. The result is a slightly ambiguous word that has the connotations of binding to the sacred and reverence for the sacred enacted by a resolute commitment to a system.

While Christianity, on this definition, would seem to definitely fit the category of being a religion, there is a sense in which Jesus' approach was also a means of critiquing this type of system. In order to understand this affirmation and negation of religion, it will be helpful to introduce a Derridian reflection upon the relationship between law and justice. The law can be described, at its best, as an attempt to set out justice. For example, we may say that, for justice to be done, those who destroy private property ought to be punished. However, as soon as we try to write down what justice is in this way, we find that this written law can embody injustice. Hence we find people who have destroyed private property (such as military equipment about to be used to bomb cities) in the name of justice. Each time the law is presented with situations which it cannot cope with, it attempts to adapt to the new situation, and it is thus edited or added to. In this way the law is never complete but is always open to change in light of new situations. This means that the law, as a system that attempts to embody justice, always falls short of justice.

So what is this justice which the law attempts to articulate? For Derrida it is impossible to say what justice is, for as soon as we say what justice is, we are left with the law, and the law always falls short. The best way to describe justice, then, is similar to the way that we would describe the absence of one we love. If we are waiting for someone we love in a bar, then their absence is something that is actually present to us – unlike all the other people in the bar, the absence of the one we are waiting for is felt by us. In a similar way, our desire to put justice into words is inspired by the power of that which we love but which is not present. Yet the law can never make justice present. While justice is not present to us, it exerts a power over us, for it is the power of this absence which causes us to attempt to transform the law and improve democracy. So then there is a very strange relationship between the law and justice: the law testifies to justice and is inspired by justice, yet justice is not found in the law. Justice cannot be spoken, for as soon as it is put into words it is unable to do justice to all. We have arrived too late for the first coming of justice and too early for the second coming.

In a similar manner we can speak of the relation between God and the Christian religion. Our religious tradition testifies to God and is inspired by God, yet our religious traditions do not make God present. Our religion is like the clearing in a forest after a great fire. It testifies to the happening of a great event and without the clearing we would not know of that event, but the clearing does not hold that event. One of the drawbacks concerning the image of a forest fire (there will always be drawbacks when we revert to images in order to bring clarity) is that it gives the impression that the poverty of religion comes from the actual absence of God. Rather, Christianity testifies to the impossibility of grasping God because of the hyper-presence of God. While the Christian is one who exists between two incomings, looking back to one in love and looking forward to the other with longing, the current moment is claimed to be awash with the Spirit. There is a certain uncertainty between these two ideas of God as absent and God as hyper-present, and no apologetic discourse can offer a way of resolving which is the case. The affirmation that religion is exposed as poverty-stricken in the hyper-presence of God (rather than in the absence of God) is a belief that is open to question.

And so, while we can say that Christianity is a religion insomuch as it binds us to the sacred enacted by fidelity to a system of belief, Christianity at its origin also signals a cutting loose from such systems via an understanding of God as transcendent – not in the modern rendering that would use this term as a means of saying that God is bigger than we are, but in the more ancient meaning of God as Wholly Other. This double act of binding to God and loosing from God that is evidenced in Christianity is one of its great strengths, for not only does it acknowledge the centrality of religion, but it also acknowledges its redundancy. The Christian religion thus testifies to a relation with God that exists without relation, to religion as both im/possible and un/necessary.

Desire for transformation and transformative desire

The net result of this understanding of the Christian religion is a very different approach to the idea and ideal of religious fulfilment. While God is impossible to grasp, this does not mean that God has no impact in our lives, for in religion we are transformed by our desire for God. In an important sense it is the inverse of how death affects us. Death is never experienced, for death is a term that refers to the end of all experience. Regardless of what, if anything, happens after this event, death has not been directly experienced by anyone who is currently reading this book. We cannot imagine what it would be like to have no consciousness, for to think about the end of consciousness is to engage in a conscious act – death is thus utterly foreign to us and impossible to imagine.

Yet, although imagining death is impossible, this does not mean that it has no effect in the present. For the great philosopher Martin Heidegger, it is only in realizing that we are moving towards death that we can become authentic human beings, for once we realize that we are going to die, we take more responsibility over our life. For instance, people who have narrowly avoided death will often feel the wonder of life in a deeper way than ever before. In the aftermath of such an experience people will often try to fix broken relationships and perhaps even try to engage in more meaningful activities. As we can see in this example, something which we cannot grasp, like death, can still have a powerful influence over us. In religious terms, we may say that the desire for spiritual transformation is not satisfied in religious commitment but rather is itself the means of spiritual transformation. In order to understand this, let us consider the following fable:

There was once a princess who grew up in a kingdom that had been ravished by decades of famines, war and plague. One night, as the princess slept she had a dream. In this dream she was walking through the market that lay by the sea, when a young beggar caught her eye. As she turned to face him the young beggar looked up, but before their eyes could meet the dream ended and the princess awoke. As the dream faded a haunting voice arose in her mind that informed her that if she were ever to meet this young man, he would shower her with riches beyond her wildest dreams.

This dream etched itself so deeply on the princess that she carried the vision deep in her heart, until one day, years later, as she walked through the market, her gaze caught hold of the same man who had visited her in her dreams all those years ago. Without pausing she ran up to him and proceeded to relay the whole vision. Never once did he look up, but when the princess had finished her story he reached into an old sack and pulled out a package. Without saying a word, he offered it to the princess and asked her to leave.

Once the princess reached her dilapidated castle she ripped open the package and, sure enough, there was a great wealth of pure gold and precious diamonds. That night she placed the package in a safe place and went to bed. But her mind was in turmoil and the long night was spent in sleepless contemplation. Early the next morning she arose, retrieved the treasures and went down to the water's edge. Once there she summoned up all her strength and threw the riches deep into the sea. After watching the package sink out of sight, she turned and without looking back went searching for the young beggar.

Finally she found him sitting in the shade of an old doorway. The princess approached, held out her hand and placed it under his chin. Then she drew his face towards hers and whispered, 'Young man, speak of the wealth you possess which allows you to give away such worldly treasure without a moment's thought.'

In this story, which charts a transformation from desire for worldly wealth into a desire for spiritual wealth, we are not told what the young man said in response to the princess's request. However, we could perhaps imagine him informing the princess that no response is necessary, for the princess's question, 'Tell me of the wealth that you possess which allows you to give away such worldly treasure without a moment's thought', can be answered with the words, 'Why, the same wealth that has allowed you to give away such worldly treasure without a moment's thought.'

This story shows how the princess's love and desire for spiritual transformation was itself spiritually transformative. The desire *for* transformation was itself the means *of* transformation: the seeking after spiritual wealth was itself the evidence of this wealth's presence. Such a strange logic is also to be found at work when we look at religious desire.

Because God, as hypernonymous, can never be made utterly present, desire is never satisfied in God. This is very different from how desire generally operates. For instance, if we desire a new car, the desire is fulfilled in its possession: what was previously absent has been made present and thus has satisfied the void which desire had formed. However, God is never made present in this way: God's presence is always hyper-presence. This is analogous to the idea of a ship sunken in the depths of the ocean: while the ship contains the water and the water contains the ship, the ship only contains a fraction of the water while the water contains the whole of the ship. Our saturation by God does not merely fill us but also testifies to an ocean we cannot contain. Thus desire for God is born in God.

This is not wholly dissimilar to the desire we experience for ones whom we love, for what we know of our beloved is but a fragment that testifies to that which lies beyond us. As relationships develop the type of desire at work changes. Let us take the example of someone who is simply seeking a relationship because they are lonely. Here they do not desire a specific individual but rather desire a certain type of individual. This type of desire is self-centred insomuch as one has self-interested reasons for seeking the relationship. However, once one is in a loving relationship, this abstract desire for a faceless some-one (who fulfils certain needs) is transformed into a concrete desire for that particular individual (beyond the simple fulfilment of those needs). The abstract, self-interested desire for another that arises from a sense of lack is transcended by a concrete desire that arises from the presence of a particular person. This, however, does not mean that the original desire is by-passed: rather, it is taken up and transformed within the new desire. Instead of our desire being satisfied in the one we love, our desire is both maintained and satisfied by and in our longing. In love we desire our beloved, indeed the presence of our beloved is that which sparks the desire. This is because the presence of the one we love testifies to the fact that what we know of them is only a fragment of what is still to be discovered. This helps us understand why Augustine said, 'For certainly nothing can be loved unless it is known.'[52] Hence we see here that seeking God is not some provisional activity which precedes the goal of finding, but is itself evidence of having already found.

Rather than desire being fulfilled in the presence of God, religious desire is born there. In short, a true spiritual seeking can be understood as the ultimate sign that one already has that which one seeks, or rather, that one is already grasped by that which one seeks to grasp. Consequently a genuine seeking after God is evidence of having found. Of course, much desire that appears to seek after God is nothing of the sort. For instance, to seek God for eternal life is to seek eternal life, while to seek God for a meaningful existence is to seek a meaningful existence. A true seeking after God results from an experience of God which one falls in love with for no reason other than finding God irresistibly lovable. In this way the lovers of God are the ones who are most passionately in search of God.

Thus the emerging community celebrate the centrality of religious desire, acknowledging that it is a necessary part of faith. This approach can help us to appreciate why the psalmist writes, 'those who *desire* God lack no good thing' and why the Gospels tell us to '*seek* first the kingdom'. Here seeking and desiring are placed over and against having and possessing. Indeed, the idea of asking, seeking and knocking as steps towards receiving, finding and a door being opened is misleading and can lead to the notion that they are two separate moments. Hence we can ask what happens if someone is seeking God yet dies before finding God. However, the verse which speaks of this (Matthew 7.7–8) does not refer to two separate moments but rather to a type of present-continuous tense by which the seeking is the finding, the asking is the receiving and the knocking is the opening – in short, these are not two distinct events but rather occur at one and the same time. Just as space and time are not distinct from each other, neither are asking and receiving.

The God-shaped hole

This leads to a very different understanding of the Pascalian phrase 'God-shaped hole'. Traditionally the God-shaped hole has referred to a type of void in every human which remains unfilled until filled by

God. This is caricatured in an urban myth that tells us of a children's address in which the minister, as part of the sermon, asked the gathering of girls and boys 'What is small, furry, climbs trees and eats nuts?' As soon as he had finished the question, a little girl stood up and said, 'Mister, I know the answer is Jesus, but it sure sounds like a squirrel.'

Here we see an extreme example of the idea that beneath the surface of daily life we all share a fundamental religious longing to which the only legitimate response is a relationship with Jesus. In Albert Camus' *The Outsider*, we are confronted with a stark rejection of this idea. Camus presents us with a self-aware character who appears to have no sense of this void. Even upon facing the cold fact of his fast-approaching execution, this character feels no desire for God. This man, Meursault, inhabits a universe in which such speculation is existentially irrelevant and meaningless. Near the end of the book he is in prison awaiting his execution. Although he has refused to see the prison chaplain on numerous occasions, the chaplain finally pays Meursault a visit anyway, and asks why he has refused to see him on previous occasions:

> I replied that I didn't believe in God. He wanted to know whether I was quite sure about that and I said I had no reason for asking myself that question: it didn't seem to matter . . . I may not have been sure what really interested me, but I was absolutely sure what didn't interest me. And what he was talking about was one of the very things that didn't interest me.[53]

In this brief exchange we are not presented with the traditional form of atheism (by which one would deny the existence of a creator). Instead Meursault has turned his back on both theism and atheism altogether, rejecting the former because it strikes him as asking a meaningless question and the latter because it takes this question too seriously. For Meursault there is no response to the spiritual question precisely because there is no question. This approach can be described as a type of quiescent anti-theism in the sense that it pays no attention to either theism or atheism.

In many ways this character can be taken to represent a contemporary response to religion, one which rejects the religious 'answer' as irrelevant precisely because the question is believed to be irrelevant. If the question has no relevance then an answer can have no purpose.

Nourished by our hunger

However, with the idea of religion as that which exists as a type of negative affirmation of God, we can say that far from having a God-shaped vacuum in our heart which remains until filled by God, the a/theology of the emerging communities allows us to turn this idea around, pointing out that far from being something that exists until being filled, the God-shaped hole can be understood as precisely that which is left in the aftermath of God.

The believer, far from once having a God-shaped hole in his or her being that is now filled, is one who has a God-shaped hole formed in the aftermath of God, a hole that compels them to seek after that which they already have. The Christian religion arises as a space that testifies to God by testifying to a God who created, but who cannot be contained, within the space. The void left by God is not unlike a type of black hole, full of something that cannot be seen and which draws our gaze into the unseen. Another analogy could be the pupil of a person's eye. This is the very place that we look at when talking to a person, the place where we encounter the other, yet this place of encounter is a black void. This is not then some kind of preference for absence over presence, seeking over finding, questions over answers or hunger over nourishment; for in the absence there is an icon to presence, in seeking there is evidence of having found, in questioning there is a hint that the answer has been given, and in hunger there is a deep and abiding nourishment. Hence, the idea that religion provides an answer can be productively challenged with the idea that it actually evokes the ultimate question – a question that places us all into question. Faith, in this rendering, can thus be described as a wound that heals.

Pascal wrote: 'Finally, let them recognize that there are two kinds of people one can call reasonable; those who serve God with all their heart because they know Him, and those who seek Him with all their heart because they do not know Him.'[54] To this we may add one caveat: that these two kinds of people are only reasonable when they are brought together as one – they serve God with all their heart because they know him, all the while seeking him with all their heart because they do not.

Being evangelized

By acknowledging these insights the emerging community is re-discovering the importance of desire and process as part of the unchanging face of Christianity. By existing in the void of hyper-presence, we discover a renewed openness to genuine dialogue with others. This dialogue replaces the standard monologue of those who would wish to either clone the other, making them into a reflection of themselves, or exclude the other, making them into a scapegoat who embodies all our fears and insecurities. Both these approaches of consumption and condemnation can be seen operating in the world today and are often reflected in one and the same organization – attempting to clone that which they simultaneously exclude as evil.

The alternative is not a relativistic acceptance of every position but rather a dialogue in which we treat everyone we meet as individuals who we can learn from and perhaps teach, rather than reducing people to the same massive and clumsy categories such as 'Christian', 'Islamic' and so on. Indeed, we see this model of treating everyone in a singular way in the life of Jesus.

One can still privilege one's own position for a whole variety of reasons. However, the difference is that those involved in the emerging conversation can engage in a genuine dialogue in which they are prepared to rethink in relation to what the other says (instead of an inauthentic dialogue in which one pretends to be open to the insights of another, but in reality one is not prepared to place one's own thinking into question). Rather than being a sign of weakness, this powerless approach is a sign of strength, for one is committed to the idea that if we genuinely seek truth from above, we will not be given a lie, for God does not give scorpions to the one who seeks bread.

In the Ikon community we have explored this idea via a group called 'The Evangelism Project'. This is a group made up largely of

Christians who seek to be evangelized and as such take time to visit other traditions within and outside Christianity. This is not an inter-faith dialogue insomuch as the group is not there to teach in any way but rather to learn. While this is a type of reverse evangelism, it has unintentionally proved to be a profoundly powerful tool for sharing Christianity with others. Generally the 'us' and 'them' approach causes both sides to solidify their thoughts and become defensive. Evangelism is usually set up as a type of debate, yet in debates we will state our views more forcibly than usual. This powerless approach breaks down the 'us' and 'them' dichotomy and provides a space in which we are all less defensive and thus more open to the work of God and the wisdom of one another. When we see our role as being not merely those who give God, but rather those who can learn from others and act as an aroma that helps others to open up (which are two sides of the same coin), then we affirm the words of Jesus when he claims that God will give God to those who are open to God.

Mission projects do not die here but, rather, are revitalized. Indeed, I have spent a lot of time with a mission group called YWAM teaching these very things. Having spoken to many of these people after their short-term mission trips, I find time and again that the idea of learning from the community that they visit enriched rather than destroyed their experience. For in this type of mission we are all transformed and have less pressure upon us to provide all the answers. In Christian mission the goal is not that some people 'out there' are brought closer to God by our work, but rather that we are all brought closer to God. Such an insight may actually help expand the numbers of people who want to be involved with mission organizations rather than diminishing them, for there are many who have been put off by the apparent superiority they are often required to assume in such environments.

Instead of bringing God to 'unreached' places and 'unreached' peoples, I find countless missionaries who say that, while this was how they once thought, time and again they find that these unreached places are the very sites where they must go to find God and to be reached. How many of us have learnt too late that our initial idea, that by serving the world we will help bring God to others, has eclipsed the wisdom that in serving the world we find God there.

Chapter 5

The third mile

—••—

Truth as soteriological event

At this point I would like to make a distinction between the idea of Truth and truth. The first, which is distinguished by the use of a capital letter, refers to the subject matter of theology and metaphysics and refers to what some philosophers have called the 'Real'. Here the word 'Real' refers to the ultimate source of everything that is. To possess some knowledge of the Truth means that one rationally accepts some propositions that accurately describe what this Real is like. Such thinking is called metaphysical because it refers to a realm that lies beyond the reach of the physical sciences, relating to questions such as the existence and nature of God, the underlying substance of the universe, the nature of logic and so forth.

In contrast to Truth, the term 'truth' can be said to relate to statements of fact concerning reality. Unlike the Real, 'reality' is a term that refers to the world as we experience it. Here metaphysical discussions are abandoned in favour of discussions concerning how we interpret and interact with the world. For instance, one may have no opinion on whether or not God exists, but one may still make meaningful statements concerning such things as the number of people who got married in a certain country at a certain time or the long-term environmental effect of carbon emissions.

The work so far may seem to suggest that Truth has no place within Christianity, for while such an approach does not deny its actual existence, the fact that Truth (God) can never be grasped ultimately leads to an eroding of absolutism that creates a space for relativism to take root. Yet one of the main problems with such a concern is the way that it presupposes a view of knowledge and truth that shares more in common with Athens than it ever did with

Jerusalem. While the above views of truth (in both its capitalized and uncapitalized forms) are important and offer a wealth of insights, these Greek-influenced approaches view questions concerning truth and knowledge in a fundamentally different manner than that found within the Judeo-Christian tradition. Rather than describing the Real or reality, the Christian idea of 'knowing the truth' can be said to operate in an entirely different realm. For, unlike the former perspectives which refer to the ability to make substantive descriptive claims concerning the Real or reality, the Judeo-Christian view of truth is concerned with having a relationship with the Real (God) that results in us transforming reality. The emphasis is thus not on description but on transformation. This perspective completely short-circuits the long-redundant debate as to whether truth is subjective or objective, for here Truth is the ungraspable Real (objective) that transforms the individual (subjective).

While the Christian can make use of these other discourses, the prime notion of truth within Christianity is directly connected with liberation and transformation rather than with objective description. For instance, when we read that Christ is the truth and that knowing the truth will set us free, we come face to face with truth, not as the objective affirmation of a proposition (as if that would set anyone free), but rather as that which arises from a life-giving encounter. The Truth in Christianity is not described but experienced. This is not then the affirmation of some objective description concerning Truth but rather describes a relation with the Truth. In other words, Truth is God and having knowledge of the Truth is evidenced, not in a doctrinal system, but in allowing that Truth to be incarnated in one's life. Hence, this claim of Christ is not a way of claiming that some theoretical system will bring new life, but a way of saying that by entering into a relationship with God we will find liberation. To know the Truth is thus to be known and transformed by the Truth. In the Epistle of John we find an extrapolation of this theme when we read that knowledge of God is evidenced in a life of love rather than in the affirmation of a theoretical, dogmatic system:

> Dear friends, let us love one another, for love comes from God. Everyone who loves has been born of God and knows God. Whoever

does not love does not know God, because God is love . . . No-one has
ever seen God; but if we love one another, God lives in us and his love
is made complete in us . . . God is love. Whoever lives in love lives in
God, and God in him.[55]

Here John equates the existence of religious knowledge with the act
of love. Knowledge of God (the Truth) as a set of propositions is utterly
absent; instead he claims that those who exhibit a genuine love know
God, regardless of their religious system, while those who do not love
cannot know God, again regardless of their religious system. Truth
is thus understood as a soteriological event. This word 'soteriological' is derived from the term *soteria*, from which we get the word
'salvation'. In precise terms the word refers to a cure, remedy or
healing.

While this religious idea of truth as soteriological may initially
seem somewhat unrelated to the idea of truth as that which describes,
there are times when they can come into conflict with each other. For
example, let us imagine that we are hiding some Jews in our house
in Germany during the Second World War. Early one morning some
soldiers come to our door as part of a routine check and ask if we are
housing any Jews. In response to this question we have three options:
(a) we regretfully say 'yes', acknowledging that we are held under a
higher moral law which requires that we do not deceive; (b) we say
'no', judging that it is the lesser of two evils, a necessary lie required
in order to prevent murder; (c) we say 'no' and feel happy that we
told the truth.

In this example most contemporary Christians in the West
would, I suspect, choose (b) as closest to their own position. However, if we take truth to mean any act which positively transforms
reality, rather than describes reality, then there is no problem
acknowledging that, while denying there are Jews in the house is
empirically incorrect, it is true in a religious sense precisely because
it protects the innocent (as well as protecting the soldiers from com-
mitting a horrific act). I have been told that the Christian writer Corrie
ten Boom was actually faced with this situation and chose to say that
there were Jews in the house. The soldiers thought she was joking and
laughed. In response to this Corrie ten Boom also laughed, and the

soldiers left. Yet, if this is a true rendering of what transpired, far from being a defence of (a), Corrie ten Boom's response is actually a perfect example of position (c), for if she was not being deceptive, then, after they had all laughed, she would have said, 'No, honestly, there are Jews in my house.' To think that this action is not a lie is somewhat equivalent to a child who, after having been told that she is not allowed out of her bedroom door all night, climbs out the window with the internal justification that this was not prohibited and thus was not wrong.

The idea that religious truth transforms reality in such a way that it reflects the kingdom of God renders some Bible stories far more intelligible, for throughout the text there are instances in which the people of God seemingly lie (i.e. say something which is empirically false) for the sake of truth. For example, at the beginning of Exodus we read of two Egyptian midwives who refuse to carry out Pharaoh's command that all male infants be put to death. Here we read:

> The king of Egypt said to the Hebrew midwives, whose names were Shiphrah and Puah, 'When you help the Hebrew women in childbirth and observe them on the delivery stool, if it is a boy, kill him; but if it is a girl, let her live.' The midwives, however, feared God and did not do what the king of Egypt had told them to do; they let the boys live. Then the king of Egypt summoned the midwives and asked them, 'Why have you done this? Why have you let the boys live?' The midwives answered Pharaoh, 'Hebrew women are not like Egyptian women; they are vigorous and give birth before the midwives arrive.' *So God was kind to the midwives and the people increased and became more numerous.*[56]

Here God does not merely accept the deception of Shiphrah and Puah but actually blesses it. Not only do we find other examples littered throughout the Old Testament, we even find Jesus himself engaged in what would appear to be an act of deception. In John 7 we read that Jesus' brothers attempt to persuade him to attend the Feast of Tabernacles. In response to this request Jesus replies:

> 'The right time for me has not yet come; for you any time is right. The world cannot hate you, but it hates me because I testify that what it does is evil. You go to the feast. I am not yet going up to this feast,

because for me the right time has not yet come.' Having said this, he stayed in Galilee. However, after his brothers had left for the feast, he went also, not publicly but in secret.[57]

The prejudice of love

Such an approach opens up a way of thinking that challenges the manner in which we have been taught to think through moral questions. Most of us have been brought up to think that Jesus taught an ethical system for his disciples to follow. The term 'ethics' refers to an approach to moral situations in which we work out how we ought to act by deriving ideas from a foundation given by reason and/or revelation. By seeing Jesus as an ethical teacher we approach the Bible as this foundation and read it as one would read a textbook – attempting to read it in a neutral manner so as to work out how we should act. In this approach we must endeavour neither to read into the text nor to interpret it, but rather to draw out from the text its precise meaning.

However, the religious idea of truth, as expressed above, places this modernistic approach into question. For, not only is there no such thing as a neutral interpretive space, but also the religious idea of truth demands that we *should* have a prejudice when reading the text: a prejudice of love. The Bible itself teaches us that we must not enter into any situation in a neutral and objective manner, even the reading of scripture, but always with eyes of love. Christ himself expressed this when he healed on the Sabbath, informing those who sought to condemn him that the law was made for humanity, not humanity for the law. Here the work of healing was judged to be more important than the dominant interpretation of the law that forbad work, precisely because healing was the loving thing to do. Here Jesus did not approach the law in a neutral manner, for the law of God was never made to be read in this way. Rather, Jesus showed that we must read it with a prejudice towards love. This does not mean that we re-interpret our traditions in any way we want, but rather that we must be committed to living in the tension between exegesis (by which we extract meaning from the text) and eisegesis (by which we read meaning into the text). By acknowledging that all our readings are located in a cultural context and have certain prejudices, we understand that engaging with the Bible can never mean that we simply extract meaning from it, but also that we read meaning into it. In being faithful to the text we must move away from the naïve attempt to read it from some neutral, heavenly height and we must attempt to read it as one who has been born of God and thus born of love: for that is the prejudice of God. Here the ideal of scripture reading as a type of scientific objectivity is replaced by an approach that creatively interprets with love.

Infinite readings and transfinite readings

In response to this, the question can be asked concerning how we ought to interpret the Bible, once we recognize that all our readings are influenced by such things as cultural context, church tradition, psychological make-up and educational background. This question revolves around the concern that once we recognize the reality that none of us merely 'translates' the Bible, but interprets it in a variety of ways, we can no longer decide which reading is good and which reading is not.

In order to answer this, we need to reflect upon two important concepts – the 'transfinite' and the 'infinite'. Infinity is a term used to describe the set of numbers that never ends, while the transfinite signals the infinite range of numbers that exists between finite numbers (e.g. between the numbers 1 and 2 we have 1.1, 1.2, 1.3 *ad infinitum*). While we must acknowledge that the Bible holds such a wealth of meaning that it can be read in a never-ending number of ways, this does not mean that it can be read in an infinite number of ways. To return to the example of an artwork, a painting can be read in multiple ways, but there are limits to the range of legitimate interpretations one can have. For instance, an image of two people embracing cannot be legitimately thought of as an image of war. In this way a piece of art has a *transfinite set of interpretations* rather than an *infinite set of interpretations*. The same goes with the Bible. While people will understand the phrase 'God is love' differently, depending upon their cultural context, it cannot be legitimately understood as a call to hate or do violence to others. So then, acknowledging that we all get God wrong and that revelation can be interpreted in a variety of ways does not necessarily mean that we are caught in the tentacles of relativism, but rather can open up a dynamic, kinetic relationship with the text.

With this in mind, we must grasp that the central interpretive tool that Jesus employed when interpreting the scriptures was the prejudice of love: he exhibited this prejudice when interpreting them in relation to his concrete interaction with those who were poor, weak and marginalized. He thus remained faithful to the text by reading it with the poor, weak and marginalized in mind. Failure to engage in this loving prejudice towards the poor can result in readings from power, readings in which we legitimate our own desires over and above the needs of those around us.

At their best, our traditions provide us with appropriate ways to engage with the various commonplace situations that arise in daily life. However, there are a myriad situations that arise in life which have not been directly faced in the past. These events often require a response which cannot be discerned via reference to our already existing interpretive maps, and instead demand a step of creative and loving interpretation. For instance, the advances in life-saving technology in the late twentieth century have cast up numerous problems in medical ethics to which no Bible passage can give a definitive answer. When thinking of this Christlike prejudice of love, I am reminded of the Buddhist story in which a disciple plucks up courage to point out to the Buddha that some of the things he taught were not in the scriptures. In response the Buddha replied, 'Then put them in.' After an embarrassed silence the disciple spoke again: 'May I be so bold as to suggest, sir, that some of the things you teach actually contradict the scriptures?' To which the Buddha, without hesitation, smiled and said, 'Then I suggest you take them out.'[58]

There is a Christlike depth to this parable that few of us will allow ourselves to perceive. Yet we can see this at work, not only within the biblical text itself, where images of God are sometimes developed, and even abandoned in favour of others, but also in more recent times. Take, for example, the issue of slavery, which, although condoned within both the Old and New Testaments (explicitly in the former and implicitly in the latter), was eventually judged by many

Christians to be a grave social evil that could not be abolished via the traditional way of interpreting scriptures. The slave was experienced as one to whom we were obliged; their suffering impinged upon us, requiring that the existing interpretations of the law be reinterpreted for the sake of justice. This reinterpretation of the law was often done by those who loved Christ and sought to follow the trajectory of Christ's teaching, for Jesus taught us not merely to read the scriptures, but to enter into a dialogue with them: a dialogue that is saturated and directed by love. The end result is a faith that engages in a double hermeneutic by which we read both our religious tradition and the situation we find ourselves in. This can be illustrated in the following story:

> The commander of the occupation troops said to the mayor of the mountain village, 'We know you are hiding a traitor. Unless you give him up to us, we shall harass you and your people by every means in our power.'
>
> The village was, indeed, hiding a man who seemed good and innocent and was loved by all. But what could the mayor do now that the welfare of the village was at stake? Days of discussion in the village council led to no conclusion. So the mayor finally took the matter up with the priest. Priest and mayor finally came up with a text that said 'It is better that one man die to save the nation.'
>
> So the mayor handed over the innocent man, whose screams echoed throughout the village as he was tortured and put to death.
>
> Twenty years later a prophet came to that village, went right up to the mayor, and said, 'How could you have done this? That man was sent by God to be the saviour of this country. And you handed him over to be tortured and killed.'
>
> 'But where did I go wrong?' pleaded the mayor. 'The priest and I looked at the scriptures and did what they commanded.'
>
> 'That's where you went wrong,' said the prophet. 'You should have also looked into his eyes.'[59]

Here the prophet in the story advocates a double hermeneutic which acknowledges that our reading of the Bible (as mediated through our particular tradition) must be re-examined and wrestled with repeatedly as we encounter the situations that present themselves to us. It is in the midst of this double reading between our interpretation of the text and our interaction with the other that the Christian community operates.

One of the most powerful and controversial cinematic explorations of this double reading is found in Costa-Gavras' film *Amen*. The film itself explores the failure of the Catholic and Protestant Churches when confronted with the terror of the death camps during the Second World War. We are presented with two religious figures, a Protestant youth pastor (Ulrich Tukur) and a Catholic priest (Mathieu Kassovitz), who each attempt to inform their respective religious leaders about the genocide. In response the churches struggle to retain their ignorance of the situation, wishing to keep their innocence by closing their eyes to the horror.

The response of the priest is of particular interest. At one point he wonders aloud to the Cardinal (Michel Duchaussoy) whether it would be possible for every Christian in Germany to convert to Judaism in order to stop the horror, for the Nazis couldn't possibly condemn such a huge number of powerful and socially integrated people at that stage in the war. The idea is, of course, utterly rejected. Then, in complete frustration, and with a crushing sense of obligation towards the persecuted, the priest takes his own advice. In tears he turns from that which he loves more than life itself – his own faith tradition – and becomes a Jew. By taking on the Jewish identity he suffers with the persecuted, voluntarily taking his place on the trains that run to Auschwitz.

For this priest, the singularity of the horror required an unprecedented action, one which cut at the heart of his tradition. It was his very tradition (or rather his interpretation of that tradition) that demanded that he should give up that tradition. This is a stunning exploration of what is demanded in the face of unprecedented horror. For most Christians, the question, 'Would you die for your beliefs?' is the most radical one that can be asked – to which the faithful will answer with a defiant 'Yes.' But *Amen* asks a more radical question, namely, 'Would you kill your beliefs?' In other words, would you be prepared to give up your religious tradition in order to affirm that tradition? Can you give up the very thing you would die to protect, not because of something even more powerful, but rather because of another's suffering?

The most powerful way for this priest to affirm his Christianity is to lay it down – symbolized by the incongruous image in which he remains in his cassock while wearing the Star of David. Here, the beliefs and practices which have served him in daily life are placed into question by the terror that faces him and the demand for a response. Amidst the fires of the Jewish persecution his Christian beliefs are subverted by the belief that Christ gave up all for the powerless. And so this priest gives up his Christianity precisely in order to retain his Christianity. It is the very narrative that he loves which requires this exodus from the narrative – losing his soul while perhaps, unintentionally, finding it.

Ethics and love

It is this double reading that ensures that we are never absolved from the difficult job of making moral decisions. The double reading requires not only a commitment to listening to and serving the people we meet, but also a deep respect for the Christian tradition. We must engage with our religious tradition, for it acts as a compass that enables us to navigate the world. Yet we must combine this compass reading with a knowledge of the terrain in which we find ourselves and a deep love in order to work out which way we must travel. Our interpretations of the Bible must then be understood more as temporary shelters than eternal structures. We never finish reading the Bible but always find ourselves standing on its threshold, ready to read again. Thus we can never rest easy, believing that we have discovered the foundations that act as a key for working out what we must do in different situations: for the only clear foundation laid down by Jesus was the law of love. This love demands that we use the scriptures not as an ethical textbook but rather as a text that extrapolates the Christlike way of being in the world.

In order to grasp what this means, let us reflect on the following teaching of Jesus: 'If anyone forces you to go one mile, go with them two miles.'[60] This teaching refers to a part of Roman law at that time which allowed a Roman soldier to compel a citizen to carry his military pack for one mile. Let us imagine that after Jesus offered this teaching to the Church, the leaders had enshrined this second-mile command into a law which stated that, if anyone was forced to carry a pack one mile, they would carry it for two miles. Then let us imagine Jesus returning to this community a few years later. Would he say to them, 'Well done, my good and faithful servants, for you have faithfully carried out my commandment', or would he perhaps shake his head and say, 'Dear friends, your law says carry the pack two miles – I say, carry it three'? If we are more drawn to the first response, then we are affirming that the teachings of Jesus are a type of ethical rulebook that must be followed in their substance; if we are drawn by the second, we are affirming that Jesus came to teach us a way of life that is dictated by the radical excess of love rather than an ethical rulebook.

Here we can see the heart of the Christian critique of ethics at work. 'Ethics', as we have already mentioned, is a word used to describe a foundational approach to moral questions which uses a set of principles (derived from reason and/or revelation) in order to work out what to do in any given situation. Far from teaching an ethical system, this was the very approach that Jesus critiqued when he called the Pharisees whitewashed tombs: clean on the outside but rotting on the inside. For ethical systems allow us to follow rules whether we love or not. While ethics says, 'What must I do in order to fulfil my responsibility?' love says, 'I will do more than is required.' If, for instance, it was the right thing to do to buy a flower on Valentine's Day for your beloved, then love says, 'I will buy more than one.' Love is never satisfied by what is required but must always do more. If ethical duty requires that we give ten per cent of our money away, then love will always look to give more than this. In this way love fulfils the *telos* (goal) of ethics by existing as the excess of ethics.

From knowledge to love: reading from right to left

In the same way that contemporary religious thought has set transcendence in opposition to immanence, and has considered theism to be the binary of atheism, so 'orthodoxy' has been interpreted as necessarily excluding heresy. Orthodoxy (a word derived from *ortho*, meaning 'correct', and *doxa*, meaning 'belief') is generally understood as referring to the embracing of right belief and thus has the connotations of that thinking which claims that we can extract substantive ethical foundations from the Bible. However, there is another way of understanding the word 'orthodoxy', one that does not set it in a binary opposition with heresy but embraces the idea that we all get God wrong.

In order to discover this alternative reading, we must break down the word 'orthodoxy' into its Greek roots, *ortho* (right) and *doxa* (belief), and read them as if one were reading Hebrew – that is, from right to left. Thus 'right belief' becomes 'believing in the right way'. Thus we break down the binary opposition between orthodoxy and heresy by understanding the term 'orthodox' as referring to someone who engages with the world in the right way – that is, in the way of love. Here religious knowledge is not something that is opposed to love, nor secondary to it; rather, the only religious knowledge worth anything *is* love. By understanding orthodoxy in this manner, it is no longer distanced from what the liberation theologians call 'orthopraxis'. Like orthodoxy, this term is often read straightforwardly as right (*ortho*) practice (*praxis*). However, once we understand orthopraxis as 'practising in the right way', we see that these two terms really shed slightly different light on the same fundamental approach. This means that the question, 'What do you believe?' must always be accompanied by the question, 'How do you believe?' We are left then with the idea of orthodoxy and orthopraxis as two terms which refer to a loving engagement with the world that is mediated, though not enslaved by, our reading of the Bible.

We can see an embodiment of this approach to orthodoxy in a situation I once found myself in, where two people from the same church, at different times, approached me to ask if I thought that their church taught the truth. The first person to ask me was a kind and gracious individual who gave of his time and money in a sacrificial manner. The church was not only a comfort to him but also a place of challenge and critique. I listened for a while before saying that I thought his church did emanate truth. Within weeks of this conversation, I met the second person. It was obvious when talking to him that his experience of the same church had been very negative. The teaching was dead to him and the type of projects which the church engaged in had done little to challenge or encourage this individual to live in a genuinely sacrificial manner. Here I found myself saying that this church did not emanate truth (at least for him).

This makes little sense within a modernist paradigm, for the idea of affirming a church as true includes the idea that you think that church is true for all, and to think that one church teaches the truth implies that you necessarily judge any church which contradicts its teaching as incorrect. Yet this need not be the case, as we can illustrate via the parable in which two camels are being led to market. One camel is loaded down with salt while the other is weighed down with cotton. On the way to the market they encounter a river which has burst its banks from a rainstorm the night before and has flooded the road. At one particularly deep part the camels are almost completely submerged. When they finally get to the other side, the camel with the salt on its back has gained a renewed sense of strength, as the water has largely dissolved the salt. However, the camel with the cotton collapses in exhaustion, for the cotton has absorbed much of the water.

In this parable we see how the same stream was experienced in two markedly different ways that depended upon the burdens that each camel brought to it. In the same way, one church may help one person to become more Christ like, while oppressing another: the idea of a single congregation being judged right or wrong in some universal way is naïve. Yet this is not an apology for relativism, because in the same way that we see the first camel as having had a better experience of the water because it is freed from a heavy load, so we must judge our various traditions according to whether they tend towards freeing their congregation from their burdens, helping to transform them into more Christlike individuals. However, if a church is not helping in our transformation, then the problem need not be the church's, or our own; rather, this may simply be the wrong context for us to be in. Rather than encouraging people to join our community (whatever 'our' community happens to be), we ought to be trying to help people to find the right community that will aid them in their further conversion.

Faith and works

If this double reading of the Bible and the other is motivated by an underlying love, then we can ask how we are supposed to justify this prejudice over any other that we might arbitrarily choose. The answer to this question is at first frustrating, for there is no way to justify the prejudice of love over any other. However, this is far from devastating, for love cannot and ought not to be justified. There is no justification for love, for if there were, then it would not be love. If we love because we are compelled through force, then it is not love. If I give some money to the poor only because someone is holding a gun to my head and demanding the action, then this is not a loving action. Neither is it loving if I act in order to gain a reward, even if the reward is simply the feeling that comes from doing the act. As soon as we say that we *should* love, then love disappears, for love is the law that has no law, the way that knows no 'should'. Love is the law that tells us when to subvert the law, when to obey the law and when to break with laws, yet love is a lawless law that cannot be argued for.

This means that my argument for love can in no way be taken as a justification for works-based salvation, for as soon as love works in order to receive something, it is not love. Love acts because it is compelled by love, not for a place in heaven. Here the binary between faith and works is devastated, as the work of love is faith by another word. The love that Christ spoke of is born of God, and when we see it at work, we know that the person has been born of God. If the works being carried out are for other reasons (such as the desire for salvation), then it is not love that we are witnessing. This love is not the narcissistic love that we see all around us and within us; this love is more radical that we can ever imagine.

Acts of love

The problem we all face when confronted by this idea of love is whether we have ever done anything that could be described as loving in the way of love that emanates from God. For when we acknowledge that true love offers everything as a gift rather than as an exchange (where we selfishly expect something in return), then we must wonder if we have ever really given a gift. To take a concrete example of what I mean, let us reflect upon how a loving relationship between two people will exhibit itself in the offering of unconditional presents. Yet in reality we often give to our beloved, not unconditionally, but with many conditions. Perhaps we give so as to get a present in exchange, but more often the return will be something much more subtle, such as a warm sensation that comes with buying a gift for our beloved, or the psychological well-being that accompanies the thanks we receive in return. We can perceive the conditional nature of our gifts most clearly whenever our relationships break down. Here we often witness people demanding that letters, photographs or presents should be given back. This behaviour is stark evidence that these things were never unconditional gifts, but rather, were given on the condition that the recipient of the gifts would continue to love the giver in return. Yet true love gives without regret and without strings.

We could perhaps say that a gift is purer when the person who receives it doesn't know who gave it. Such anonymous presents do not present the danger of the selfish pleasure that arises from getting thanks from the one who is receiving the gift. However, there is still the joy of knowing that the recipient is grateful to someone (a thought that can give us great pleasure) and that we have made that person happy. A good friend of mine once bought me tickets to see my favourite band in concert and posted them anonymously through my door. Only years later, by chance, did I find out who had done this. While this was a beautiful gesture, he admitted that the act had given him a deep sense of pleasure at imagining my surprise and delight.

So perhaps an even purer gift would not only be one that was given anonymously but one where nothing was actually given. In this way the person would not be thankful to anyone, for they would not have actually received anything at all. This may seem very strange at first, but we can use the example of one person offering forgiveness to another. If someone wrongs me without knowing and I later say that I have forgiven them, then I have offered a gift which is literally nothing, for forgiveness is not a thing. However, giving this type of gift can often be very rewarding on a personal level, for I may be seeking an apology in return, may want to look spiritual or may have the desire that my apology be humbly accepted. As such, it is important that we should sometimes endeavour to offer the gift of forgiveness without the other person even knowing. Here we do not get the warm feeling of them knowing that we have done such an act, nor the pleasure of knowing that they are happier as a result, and thus the act of offering forgiveness is purer.

However, a gift in which the receiver does not know who the giver is, or even that they have received a gift, still has the problem of the person feeling good about themselves: thinking, for instance, that they are spiritual enough to do such a selfless act. Here the gift has a return of pride and self-satisfaction. And so Derrida, to whom I am grateful for helping me reflect on the idea of gift, claimed that the perfect gift would have a third criteria: namely that the giver would not know that he or she had given it. Here we are presented with three criteria for the perfect, loving gift – that is, one that we would not use in order to get a reward: (1) the receiver does not know he or she has been given a gift; (2) nothing is actually given; and (3) the giver does not know he or she has given anything.

At first this sounds both impossible and ridiculous. However, it is here that we gain an insight into what Christian giving actually looks like. For a love that is born from God is a love that gives with the same reflex as that which causes a bird to sing or the heart to beat. For a concrete example of this, we can say that an act of love could involve giving money to someone on the street without stopping to think, or talking to someone who is in pain without thought that we are doing anything special or different from any other daily activity. Is this not what is really meant by the biblical injunction to give so as the right hand does not know what the left has given? The love that arises from God is a love that loves anonymously, a love that acts without such self-centred reflections, that gives without thought. Our lives should be full of acts of love of this kind, and yet, by definition, they will be invisible to us. As Meister Eckhart once said:

> When one can do the works of virtue without preparing, by willing
> to do them, and bring to completion some great and righteous
> matter without giving it a thought – when the deed of virtue seems to

happen by itself, simply because one loved goodness and for no other reason, then one is perfectly virtuous and not before.[61]

Yet here is the difficult bit, for we cannot force this radical, Christlike love, we cannot work it up or commit to living in this way. We cannot read this chapter and then say, 'OK, today I will live this life of love', for that would not be the life of love, it would be forced and would lead to condemnation and/or arrogance. So what can we do?

Letting go

This underlying love cannot be worked up but is gained only as we give up. To be born of God is to be born of love. Here we come into contact again with Meister Eckhart, who claims that we must let go of ourselves in such a manner that we can become a dwelling place in which God can reside and from which God can flow. Our own works and beliefs are here dethroned by the enthronement of God. What is important for Eckhart is not to think correctly, or to work hard, but rather to engage in a type of concrete ego-death by which the divine is invited to enter the place which we have laid down. The hope is that in so doing, love will flow from us.

And so we end Part 1 as we began, with the word 'love'. Not an inauthentic love which only embraces those who embrace us, but the love that emanates from our beloved, the love that would embrace our enemies, that gives until it hurts and then gives more, the love that gives with the right hand while hiding its gift from the left. To affirm the approach that I am advocating means that we must accept that to be a Christian is to be born of love, transformed by love and committed to transforming the world with love. This is not somehow done by working ourselves up and trying to find the right way of thinking and acting, but rather in letting go and opening up to the transformative power of God. In so doing, we will not merely sit around describing God to the world, but rather, we will become the iconic spaces in which God is made manifest in the world. It is my hope and prayer that those of us taking part in this emerging conversation will find ourselves translating that dialogue into a journey that willingly walks that third mile with Christ.

Part 2

TOWARDS ORTHOPRAXIS: BRINGING THEORY TO CHURCH

In Part 1 we explored how those involved in the emerging conversation are helping to reintroduce an understanding of faith that radically critiques the 'theological' approach found in large sections of the contemporary Church. This understanding includes a rediscovery of ideas such as: concealment as an aspect of revelation; God as hyper-present; the affirmation of doubt; the place of silence; religious desire as part of faith; Christian discourse as a/theological; God-talk as iconic; a recognition of journey and becoming; truth as soteriological event; and orthodoxy as a way of believing in the right way. While it may be useful to spend the remainder of this book delving into these ideas in a more sustained and careful manner, we must bear in mind that the emerging conversation is not being undertaken by armchair academics who merely seek to interpret Christianity, but rather by activists who would wish to embody it. For as we all know, one does not learn to be a Christian, but rather, one engages in a process of becoming one. As such, the movement that is being initiated by those involved in the emerging conversation is not primarily an abstract one that has grown out of a university context, but is rather a movement concretely involved in sustaining and developing faith communities.

The theoretical considerations are still vital, for those who would shun academic insights are generally not those who are free from theory but rather the ones who are most in danger of being enslaved by it. However, we must also explore how such theory translates into a liturgical context. Part 2 is thus aimed at showing how the ideas expressed in Part 1 may be employed within a religious environment so as to help facilitate a context for personal and communal transformation.

While the following resources can be employed to aid discussion and reflection within study groups, they are primarily intended to provide a means of introducing the ideas into a liturgical environment. In order to do this, I have extracted ten services from Ikon, a group who have dedicated a great deal of time to exploring and developing the various themes we have been looking at.

What you are about to read provides a brief description of various services that this group has created. The descriptions, by necessity, are partial and do not reflect the rich use of poetry, music and discussion that is involved in each gathering. However, the core elements of each service are provided so that readers may gain some feel for the evenings. These services could not and should not be packaged as some universal product to be exported around the world. The idea that what follows can be translated without remainder across cultures and communities fails to grasp that these events are locally produced and reflect the skills and needs of a particular group. Ikon is an organic, local community that takes the skills of that community in order to serve that community. It is a regional group that reflects the unique needs of the people who attend. In short, it is not a universal model for how religious groups should be run. And so the following services seek only to offer a partial map to help the readers gain a bearing rather than tell them how to make the journey. Each chapter includes a short theoretical background to the service and a description of the evening. The hope is that this will be useful for providing some resources for those who wish to explore some of the themes we have reflected upon (expanding, changing and transforming what is contained here).

Each service is evangelical insomuch as it aims to facilitate a type of conversion amongst those who attend. However, Ikon is no crypto-evangelical mission or advanced seeker service, for this commitment to conversion is not one that is offered by 'us' to 'them' (whoever this 'them' happens to be). Rather, everyone in the bar (participants and passers by) is a potential implement of our further conversion. Consequently, the evangelical nature of the community does not resemble a one-way diatribe leading from 'us' to 'them' but rather embodies a multiple dialogue that moves from one to another.

Each service also attempts to remain faithful to the Augustinian axiom that only God gives God. Because of this the services are designed in such a way as to minimize specific doctrinal statements in favour of employing the Christian narrative to create a space for reflection and encounter. In this way Ikon resembles more an optician's surgery, which helps the eye become more receptive and sensitive to light, rather than a painter's studio, which would offer images for the sight.

While the services stand alone, I have tried to choose ones that mirror the broad trajectory at work in Part 1. We thus begin with five services that deconstruct our ideas of God in an effort to rediscover the place of mystery in faith. Accordingly, they deal with subjects such as transcendence, uncertainty, absence, openness and expectancy. The next five services focus attention on the human side of faith. Here we explore our relationship with other people via themes that include the body of Christ, confession, selfishness, judgement and love.

Service 1

'Eloi, Eloi, lama sabachthani?'

———◦•◦———

Background to the service

For the contemporary Christian it is all but impossible to reflect upon the crucifixion without simultaneously bringing to mind the resurrection. While separate temporal events, they are so irrevocably intertwined in our minds that to consider one without the other, if even possible, would seem to be tantamount to falling foul of a fundamental trespass against the radical singularity of the (two) event(s). In short, to consider the crucifixion in isolation from the resurrection would amount to fracturing the radical unity of the Easter narrative: for the crucifixion without resurrection would seem to signal the death of faith. Consequently the Easter story, if it is to be understood at all, is to be understood as an irreducibly complex singularity – to tear one part away from the whole would be to effectively destroy both the parts and the whole.

And yet such a seemingly religious approach may actually veil a dark, irreligious heart. If we consider the 2004 film *The Passion of the Christ* by Mel Gibson, we can recall that it was criticized by some for its minimal reference to the resurrection. However, let us imagine for a moment that, far from having a greater emphasis upon the resurrection, the film had ignored it entirely. Then let us consider the possibility that, rather than being something deeply inappropriate, this silence could have been the only truly appropriate end for a film exploring the nature of the cross. In contrast to those who would say that its minimal reference to Christ's return was far too small, perhaps the opposite is true: namely, that for today's audience it was far too much.

To imagine that the horror of the cross is exhausted in the physical pain or profound injustice that it symbolizes is to misunderstand the true horror of this symbol. While the image of suffering is truly harrowing, it is not the only or even the central horror of this central event. Such reflections can still offer the believer a safe, cathartic horror that is wrapped in the understanding that everything works out well in the end. In contrast to this, the true horror of the cross allows no such shelter, for if considered in itself, it signals the seeming abandonment of God by God and the possible victory of an all-embracing nihilism. Ironically, if *The Passion* had delved deeper into the heart of the cross, it may well have strategically denied the resurrection entirely, ending with a closed tomb, thereby forcing the viewer to think about their response to Christ amidst his absence and in the seeming face of his abandonment by God.

Without the closure of a resurrection, we would be presented with the unnerving question as to whether our love of Christ is really a love of ourselves, for it is at the foot of the cross that one may truly consider embracing Christianity without the comfort of thinking that such a giving of one's life is also the means of gaining it back (if one gives in order to receive, one does not really give at all but rather engages in an economic exchange). This provides the means of testing whether our faith is a gift by which we offer ourselves freely rather than an economy by which we negotiate a return.

So then, far from considering cross and resurrection as two sides of the same coin, there are times when we must be courageous enough to close our eyes and imagine the unimaginable end of God. For it is here, in this space, that the truly radical decision can be made. Faith, although not born at the crucifixion, is put on trial there.

So then, what if the only way for us to truly contemplate the horror of the cross requires that we banish all thoughts of resurrection from our mind? In other words, what if the only way for us to understand this seminal moment involves placing ourselves in the position of the original disciples, psychologically inhabiting that rarely mentioned Saturday between Good Friday and Easter Sunday?

Service description

It is the middle of winter and, while only 6.30 in the evening, it is already dark and bitterly cold. A small group of people huddle together outside a dilapidated, nondescript building that lies back from the main road. It has no windows and is located in waste ground in a bad part of the city. This is The Menagerie Bar. Those outside are waiting to be let in so that they can set up for the evening's Ikon event. They have already been waiting for 30 minutes: yet again the bar staff are late. Once more they wonder if anyone will open up – it wouldn't be the first time that the doors have remained shut and people have been sent home. However, shortly after 6.30, The Menagerie's most committed regular appears. Gerry shows up every evening the bar is open and drinks nothing but tea from opening time to closing. The appearance of this mysterious figure is a good omen and fills everyone with hope that someone is bound to arrive shortly. Sure enough, only five more minutes pass before the manager appears from around the corner, driving an old car with no front window and a smashed headlight. He greets us with a slight nod before reaching for his keys. With only 25 minutes remaining before people begin to arrive, this small group enter the bar and set to work.

Within 20 minutes the room is bathed in the light from a hundred candles, the old pinball machine has been unplugged and the stench of stale alcohol from the night before is gradually losing its battle with the sweet aroma from burning incense. A DJ stands in the far corner with his head down, playing some slow ambient beats. Every few minutes he mixes the words *'Eloi, eloi, lama sabachthani?'* into the music so that they echo faintly around the room.

By seven o'clock the first people begin to arrive. They enter quietly through the reinforced front door and descend an old staircase into the bar. The atmosphere is tense and the dark ambience created by the music gives the place a conspiratorial feel. On the dark-green walls there are dozens of Fifties pin-ups in old frames. To one side of the room a large blank canvas has been set up on an easel. A young woman is standing in front of it, expressionless, as she writes, 'My God, my God, why have you forsaken me?' repeatedly in thick black paint onto the surface.

Another ten minutes pass before the music begins to fade and a video projector at the back of the room buzzes into life. Behind the stage a huge image of Hans Holbein's *The Body of the Dead Christ in the Tomb* is projected. The ceiling of the bar is low, so the image rests at body height. There has been little attempt to clear a space for this picture of Christ's lifeless body, and so it spills over onto whatever else is on the wall. As the image is brought into focus a young man who was moments before sitting at the bar stands up and approaches a mike at the foot of the stage. He stands in front of the image, so that part of it reflects off his T-shirt, takes another sip from his drink and waits as people bring their conversations to a close. Only when there is silence does he begin to speak:

It has been said that on the day Christ was crucified a group of followers packed their few belongings and set off to find a new home. They were so distraught that they could not bear to stay in the place where Jesus had been executed. So they left, never to return, and after travelling thousands of miles, they set up an isolated village far from civilization. Once settled, they each took an oath to protect the memory of Jesus and live by his teaching.

Then one day, after 300 years of solitude, a small band of Christian missionaries reached the isolated settlement and were amazed to find a community of people living the sacrificial way that Christ had taught, yet who possessed no knowledge of his subsequent resurrection and ascension. Without hesitation the missionaries called the entire community together and taught them what had occurred after the crucifixion.

That evening there was a great celebration in the camp. Yet, as the night progressed, one of the missionaries noticed that the leader of the community was absent. This bothered the young man and so he set out to look for the community elder, whom he eventually found in a small hut on the fringe of the village, praying and weeping.

'Why are you in such sorrow?' asked the missionary in amazement. 'Today is a day for great celebration!'

'A day for great celebration and great sorrow,' replied the elder, who was all the while crouched on the floor. 'For over 300 years we have followed the ways taught to us by Christ. We followed his ways faithfully, even though it cost us deeply, and we remained resolute despite the fear that death defeated him and would one day defeat us also.'

The elder slowly got to his feet and looked the missionary compassionately in the face.

'Each day we have forsaken our very lives for him because we judge him wholly worthy of the sacrifice, wholly worthy of our being. But now I am concerned that my children and my children's children may follow him not because of the implicit value he has, but because of the value that he possesses for them.'

With this the elder left the hut and made his way to the celebration, leaving the missionary to his thoughts.

The young man pauses momentarily as the background music changes tempo and looks over to the painting that is taking shape in the corner. The canvas is gradually changing from its original white to a deep black as the words being painted melt into one another and begin to coalesce. After another 30 seconds have passed, he continues:

Here we are presented with a community who followed Christ not because of a resurrection but because of a seduction. They knew what that cry of abandonment on the cross really meant, for they had lived with it for as long as they could remember.

It is in this place of radical uncertainty that we, like this community, can ask ourselves why we are struggling to be faithful to Christ. Here we can ask whether it is because doing so offers us some meaning and security in life or whether our commitment to becoming Christian transcends this.

There is a short time of reflection as the DJ plays. After a few minutes a young woman takes the mike. She looks over those who have gathered and begins to speak:

Holy Saturday is the name that is given to that 24-hour period nestled between Good Friday and Easter Sunday, between crucifixion and resurrection.

It is a day that speaks of the absence of God and is as much a part of the Christian experience as the day before and the day after. It is the moment when we experience the depth of Christ's cry on the cross, the moment when we feel abandoned by God and utterly alone in the world. This day is never as far from us as we would wish, for there are times when we all are unsettled by the feeling that we have been abandoned and that everything we believe may be nothing more than empty words and hopeless dreams. This is the horror of the cross, not the blood and suffering of an innocent, but the removal of God.

Holy Saturday ridicules the idea that the feeling of God's absence is reserved for those who are irreligious, for in reality it is only the religious individual who can really know this absence. This is analogous to the experience of waiting for one whom we love in a café. The later they are, the more we experience their absence. Our beloved is absent to everyone in the room but we are the only one who *feels* it.

Who among us does not find ourselves dwelling, from time to time, or perhaps at all times, in the space of Holy Saturday? Yet this day is rarely spoken of and the experience is often seen as one to be avoided or merely tolerated rather than embraced.

After she returns to her seat a musician plugs her guitar into the old PA system, a loud crackle breaks through the silence and some feedback momentarily cuts through the sober atmosphere. As she tunes her guitar she takes a moment to share what this sense of divine absence has meant in her life. These words seamlessly give way to song as she begins to sing of fidelity, longing and abandonment. As in many Ikon services, there is a slight awkwardness in the room. Moments like these seem so personal and yet are played out in such a public space.

Before the service two tables had been carried onto the stage and draped with a dark-red velvet. On one of the tables a church candle burns while on the other rests a large open Bible surrounded by flowers. Once the musician finishes, the original speaker returns to the mike and begins to speak:

> In the Bible we read that while Christ hung on the cross a dark cloud engulfed him. What was this dark cloud? Did it signal the victory of nihilism or was it the dark dwelling place of God?

While he is speaking two people quietly move onto the stage and stand behind the tables. When he has finished the person who stands behind the table with the candle holds this candle above his head and begins to speak:

> There is a service in the Christian calendar called Tenebrae. When it's described, some people are surprised at its very existence, because it seems so foreign to the accepted notion of what Christian worship should be. This is not designed to be a happy service, because the occasion is not happy. If your expectation of Christian worship is that it should always be happy and exhilarating, you won't appreciate this service

until the second time you attend it. Having grown up in a Christian tradition in which it was practised, it remains very important to me.

Tenebrae is Latin for 'darkness', so it is a service of darkness. Tenebrae services are held on the night of Good Friday, and its purpose is to recreate the emotional aspects of the passion story. Specifically, Tenebrae is a Christian service with no benefits of Christ's resurrection. There is no sermon, no prayer in Jesus' name, no offering as there is no Christian work, and no benediction. There are no announcements, and there is no coffee hour. There is no chat before or after the service. It recreates the betrayal, abandonment and agony of the events of Christ's death, and it is left unfinished, because the service isn't over until Easter Day, making it technically the longest service of the Christian calendar.

At the beginning of the service, the church is lit by a number of candles, as many candles as there are readings of scripture. The readings are taken from the Gospel accounts of the last hours of Christ's life. Hymns and other pieces of music are sung, all around the theme of Christ's death. And one by one, the candles are extinguished.

As the service continues, the church becomes darker and darker. It becomes progressively difficult to see. Darkness envelops the church.

Only one candle remains. It is the Candle of Prophecy, and it is not extinguished; it symbolizes the promises that Christ will not stay dead, but that he will rise. But to those of us furtively stumbling with mincing steps towards the doors of the church, it is not much light to work with. Just as to those who stood on Golgotha, in dense darkness, watching a wailing mother holding her son's lifeless body, those ancient promises must have seemed very faint indeed. But this candle will burn, in an empty, dark church, for three days.[62]

As these words are spoken some people walk quietly around the room blowing out the candles that are dispersed around the bar until only the candle being held remains lit. At the same time the projected image of Christ gradually dims until it disappears entirely from view. The room is now bathed in darkness; the only light is that which emanates from the single candle, which the speaker sets down on the table before returning to his seat. After a brief pause the person standing behind the second table speaks:

I would like to share with you a dream I had recently, in which I found myself sitting alone in a large candlelit cathedral. As I sat there transfixed by the crucifix that hung above the altar, I remember hearing the doors of the sanctuary open. As I looked around I saw a woman dressed in black walking up the aisle crying.

Without looking at me, she approached the altar and laid some flowers beneath the crucifix. Then she went over to one of the side chapels and blew out the candles that others had lit as part of their prayers. After this she approached the lectern and closed the large Bible that rested there. As she left I awoke.

It was only later that I began to understand the symbolism of this dark vision. The woman in black was Mary. She had laid flowers at the altar for this place was the tomb of God; she had blown out the candles because no divine ear was listening to the prayers; and she had closed the Bible for the Word had been silenced.

As he finishes, he slams the Bible shut and sits down. At the same time the background music stops. The person standing at the foot of the stage (between the two altars) begins to speak again:

These two interpretations signify different ways of approaching the experience of Holy Saturday. One holds to the belief that all will be well, the other sees only the end of God. The point is not that we choose between these but that we stand resolute, regardless of which is right.

In closing, we are all asked to close our eyes before the speaker continues:

Let us imagine that we have died and are waiting to stand before the judgement seat of God . . . Try to imagine how it feels to look over your life – what you are happy about and what you regret . . . Now imagine being brought into a magnificent room within which there is a great white throne. Upon this throne is a breath-taking being who shines as if full of light . . .

After a moment the one who sits on the throne begins to speak: 'My name is Lucifer and I am the angel of light. I have cast your God from his throne and banished Christ to the realm of eternal death. It is I who hold the keys to this kingdom. I am the gatekeeper of paradise and it is for me to decide who shall enter and who shall be forsaken.'

Now imagine that this angel stretches out his vast arms and says, 'In my right hand I hold eternal life and in my left I hold death. For those who would bow down and acknowledge me as Lord, I shall grant them safe passage into paradise, but those who refuse I will vanquish to death with their Christ.'

'Eloi, eloi, lama sabachthani?'

After this the devil moves his arms so that each of his hands is placed before you and asks, 'What do you choose?'

It is only as we experience Holy Saturday that we can ask whether we would follow Christ regardless of heaven or hell, regardless of pain or pleasure, whether we would follow in the midst of the uncertainty that Holy Saturday brings to our lives. It is only here that we can ask if we have truly offered ourselves to God for no reason other than the desire to offer ourselves as a gift. Faith does not die here, rather it is forged here.

The room is silent and almost pitch black. By now the large canvas in the corner of the room is covered in multiple layers of thick black paint. There is no formal end to the service but one by one people begin to open their eyes and talk. After a few moments some candles are re-lit and the music picks up. As this is happening everyone is brought a small candle and a burnt match (each placed inside a small plastic envelope) as a symbol of the two interpretations of Holy Saturday to aid personal reflection.

Service 2

Prodigal

⟡

Background to the service

Following on from '*Eloi, Eloi, lama sabachthani?*', this service provides an opportunity to deepen the exploration of divine absence by seeing how this experience of the void does not simply arise as a rare but potent moment in faith (as in the experience of Holy Saturday) but is a sustained and subtle presence in the life of the believer. In order to understand this we must reflect upon two common ways that something can be revealed to us.

First, something can appear in an anonymous manner. Here, as we have explored in Part 1, that which reveals itself to us in this way is given in an insufficient manner. For example, if we know that a friend is waiting for us in a pub, but the lighting is insufficient to identify him or her from among the crowd, then we can say that the friend's presence is anonymous (for while there is enough light to enable us to see our friend, there is not enough light to allow us to identify him or her from the rest of the crowd).

The second common way of understanding the revelation of something can be described in terms of adequacy. That which is revealed in an adequate manner is revealed in a manner that allows us to understand it. Here we can add to the previous example by imagining that, as our eyes become accustomed to the darkness of the bar, we begin to make out the features of our friend and thus identify him or her from the crowd.

It is generally assumed by religious people today that God's revelation can be understood via anonymity and adequacy. As an example of the former, the existence and nature of the universe can be said to offer anonymous revelation, for by employing versions of

91

the teleological and cosmological arguments, it is said by some that we can make certain basic claims about the source of the universe. The believer will generally point out that this general revelation, while important, is ultimately insufficient and must be superseded by the latter type of revelation whereby God is manifest more substantially through the prophets, Jesus or some kind of personal encounter. In this way God is no longer unknown because of some lack of information, but made known through a sufficient revelation.

Yet there is a third way that something can be made manifest, and it is this third way that represents the highest mode of revelation. Here something appears in such a way that it saturates us and short-circuits our understanding. This third way is a type of super-abundant revelation that renders the thing in question hypernonymous. Hypernymity refers to a type of revelation that cannot be reduced to pure presence precisely because there is too much to grasp: there is an absolute excess of information. In this understanding, God's revelation is understood not as that which makes God present to understanding or experience, but rather as that which overcomes understanding and experience through God's superabundant presence.

In addition to the categories of 'unknown' and 'known' we must therefore add the category 'un/known'. Here the hyper-presence of God is experienced by the religious participant as a type of absence, for our minds are unable to make the God who is there intelligible to us. This third level of revelation acknowledges that while God participates with the world, God is never present to the world in the way that everyday objects are. In this third mode of revelation God's absence is seen to be a part of the experience of God's presence: not because God is truly absent but rather because God is hyper-present.

'Prodigal' explores this idea of over-abundant revelation by exploring how God's participation with the world is so luminous that all our attempts at rendering God present to the mind or experience turn out to be wounded, provisional and inadequate. By exploring how faith includes a sense of God as one who is absent (because of our inability to grasp God's presence), we explore how seeking after God is a part of what it means to have faith, rather than something that happens as a preliminary step in the move towards faith. With this in mind, 'Prodigal' aims to facilitate a space for contemplation upon the idea that our longing for God is actually a sign of God's (hyper)presence.

Service description

As usual, there is a rush to finish setting up the room before people arrive. As the doors open we are still struggling with the reliably unreliable PA system. But as people begin to order their drinks, the lights are finally dimmed and the PA kicks into life. The common purse is placed onto the bar (a basket that people can put money into and take money out of throughout the service) and the DJ begins to play.

Around the room dozens of Mills and Boon novels that we had purchased in a second-hand bookshop have been scattered around the various surfaces. A large, white, semi-permeable material dominates the room. It hangs from the ceiling in the centre of the room and is covered by a projection of Rembrandt's *Head of Christ*.

After a few more minutes have passed the music begins to fade and a man approaches the stage before waiting patiently for the room to go quiet. When the various conversations have come to an end he takes the mike and begins:

> There was once a rich and kindly father who lived with his two sons in a great gothic mansion. They had resided there together for many years until, late one evening, in the very dead of night, the father mysteriously left.
>
> Each son dealt with the horror of this loss in a different way. The eldest son ignored and suppressed the midnight exodus of his father entirely and continued with his daily chores religiously. Through toil and rationalization he repressed the haunting knowledge that his father was gone, allowing it to fester silently in the depths of his being.
>
> In contrast, the younger son was openly overcome with confusion and fear. In desperation he withdrew his inheritance and also left. He too suppressed the terror in his heart, but chose to forget by using the amnesia offered by pleasure, spending his money and time on worldly distractions. Yet the path he chose was a lonely one that led only to destitution and poverty. It wasn't long before he found himself without money or friends, working on a farm where he was forced to share the animals' food.

After many years of this pitiful existence he gathered resolution in his heart and set about the return journey to his father's home. When he finally returned to the great mansion, he found his elder brother still caring for the property, still toiling on the land and still suppressing the memory of their father's departure.

The brother who had never left held resentment in his heart against the sibling who had squandered his inheritance only to return empty-handed and broken-hearted. However, the young man paid no heed to this animosity, for his gaze was set upon a higher concern. Each day he would ready a calf for slaughter and lay out his father's favourite cloak in preparation for a great feast. Once he had completed this daily ritual he would sit by the entrance of the mansion and await his father's return.

He waits there still, to this very day, yearning for the homecoming of the prodigal father with longing and forgiveness overflowing his heart.

The parable is then followed by some poetry and music on the theme of loss and yearning. Between each piece somebody comes up to the front and shares a time in their own life when the absence of God has been most present to them. After this we are all encouraged to spend a few minutes sharing an experience of this kind with others at our table. About ten minutes pass before someone approaches the stage to speak:

We often think that desire arises from the absence of that which we seek. For instance, we long for food because we lack the nourishment that food brings and we are satisfied when we have eaten. However, in a loving relationship our desire for the other arises from their actual presence. In love the presence of the other does not fulfil our yearning, as food fulfils our hunger, but rather deepens it.

So too our religious desire is never satisfied in God but rather deepened there. We cannot grasp God, not because God is absent, but rather because God is always given in excess of our ability to grasp. It is because of this that the revelation of God is not to be thought of as the opposite of concealment but rather has concealment built into its very heart, for each revelation is so luminous that it cannot be reduced to the horizon of our sight. In this way the revelation of God is like a veil which both reveals and conceals the one whom we love.

Behind me is a projection of Rembrandt's *Head of Christ*. It is projected onto a permeable material so as to draw out how God's revelation is like a wedding veil – one which both exposes and conceals our beloved.

People are given some time to meditate on the projected image; there is some poetry and an opportunity for people to talk among themselves. After 15 minutes someone approaches the stage and speaks:

Pascal once wrote: 'Finally, let them recognize that there are two kinds of people one can call reasonable; those who serve God with all their heart because they know him, and those who seek him with all their heart because they do not know him.'[63]

But what if these two people are really only reasonable when they are thought to be two different parts of the one person? What if only those who truly serve God can really know what it is to yearn for God, and only those who truly desire God can really know what it is to serve God?

From elsewhere in the room the following verse is read from a large Bible:

Everyone who asks receives; those who seek find and to those who knock, the door will be opened.

The Bible is closed and the person at the stage continues:

Here we learn that in the very instant of asking, we receive; in seeking, we find; and in knocking, we enter. Here seeking and finding do not follow one another as day follows night but occur simultaneously, as heat emanates from light.

Perhaps, then, the secret longing for God could be the sign that God is already among us in a way that is beyond our understanding and experience. Is this not what the psalmist hints at when he says that those who desire God lack no good thing? And is this not the message of the Gospels when we read that we must seek first the kingdom of God and its righteousness? Here desiring and seeking are placed over and above having and possessing.

As the service draws to a close everyone is invited to take away a Mills and Boon book as a reminder of the evening's theme.

Service 3

Sins of the Father

———•◦•———

Background to the service

There is a pragmatic logic that advises us to avoid wrestling with a force that is vastly superior to our own. This, of course, reflects the simple wisdom of self-preservation. Yet such logic is often ignored in the Judeo-Christian scriptures, for here we encounter numerous individuals who steadfastly confront their creator. In these interactions we do not find them humbly confessing their trespasses before God, but rather accusing God of trespassing against them. This rich tradition, in which one kneels before God with a clenched fist, is not only to be found in the stories of Moses and Job, along with the Psalms, but also in the work of contemporary believers who have wrestled with the singular horror of events such as the holocaust.

These violent confrontations between creation and the creator are all the more amazing in that they are often instigated by those who are faithful friends of God. We are confronted with a vast number of believers throughout history whose deep, abiding faith has sounded like infidelity, in a manner reminiscent of Christ's cry on the cross.

The reason for this inability to comprehend such outbursts lies partly in our inability to grasp the radical nature of faith, a faith that must be marked with passion, even if that passion often seems to be directed against the source of faith. Indeed, in the book of Revelation we read that God prefers the faithful to be hot or cold rather than lukewarm. Indeed, to be 'cold' can actually be a sign that one is very close to God. For often a violent reaction against God signals the presence of God. Rather than thinking that genuine religious experience is always comforting, the sense that there is one who can see into the very depths of our being can cause us to turn and run from God. Such repulsion and fear arises from the actual experience of God, for to feel naked and ashamed before God presupposes some kind of relation with God.

Yet this does not exhaust the experience of a God-inspired reaction against God, for in the book of Job we witness a reaction against God that is linked not to our own misdeeds but to the seeming misdeeds of God. While the Bible often speaks of God as one who stands beyond all human accusations, this is held in tension with other portions of the text which testify to the human experience of a God who regrets, is jealous, angry and even indifferent to suffering. The fact that some biblical characters are portrayed as fighting against God in the name of justice shows that accusing God of wrongdoing has a place within the Judeo-Christian tradition. For, while God may ultimately stand beyond all accusations, our experience of the world can lead us to legitimately question this.

Service description

A long table has been placed along the stage. On its surface a dozen broken wine glasses rest in a bed of sand. One of the walls is covered by a large projection of the words, 'You tireless watcher of human-ity', while small slips of paper and pens sit on each table. Upon entering the room we are greeted by the music of the DJ who is looping the following words into the music:

> When I was hungry you gave me nothing to eat.
> When I was thirsty you gave me nothing to drink.
> I was a stranger and you did not invite me in.
> I needed clothes and you did not clothe me.
> I was sick and in prison and you did not look after me.

Very gradually the music dies away while these words become louder. Before long before the words begin to drown out people's conversa-tion. As the room goes silent a young man approaches the mike and, once the words have died away, he begins to speak:

> Once, a long time ago, I had the privilege of spending some time with
> an old rabbi, bent with age and way too familiar with suffering. Each
> evening he used to tell me the story of a Jew who escaped the Spanish
> Inquisition with his wife and child, making his way, in a small boat,
> across the stormy sea to a stony island. A flash of lightning exploded

and killed his wife. A whirlwind arose and hurled his child into the
heart of the sea. Alone, wretched, discarded like a stone, terrified
by thunder and lightning, his hair dishevelled, his body ravaged by
hunger and his hands raised to God, the Jew made his way up onto
the rocky desert island and turned thus to God:

'God of Israel,' he said, 'I have fled to this place so that I may serve
you in peace, to follow your commandments and glorify your name.
You, however, are doing everything to make me cease believing in you.
But if you think that you will succeed with these trials in deflecting
me from the true path, then I cry to you, my God and the God of my
parents, that none of it will help you. You may insult me, you may
chastise me, you may take from me the dearest and the best that I have
in the world, you may torture me to death – I will always believe in
you. I will love you always and forever – even despite you.

'Here, then, are my last words to you, my angry God: None of this
will avail you in the least! You have done everything to make me lose
my faith in you, to make me cease to believe in you. But I die exactly
as I have lived, an unshakeable believer in you.'

He lives to this day, that angry man with his God, on that little rocky
island located somewhere silently in our hearts. Tonight we will
endeavour to let him speak.[64]

As the music picks up someone walks to the mike and speaks the
following scriptures as a prayer:

> Am I the sea, or the wild sea beast that you should keep me under
>   watch and guard?
> Strangling I would welcome rather, and death, than these my
>   sufferings.
> Will you never take your eyes off me long enough for me to
>   swallow my spittle?
> Suppose I had sinned, what have I done to you,
> you tireless watcher of humanity?
> Why do you choose me as your target?
> Why should I be a burden to you?
> Can you not tolerate my sin, nor overlook my fault?
> It will not be long before I lie on earth;
> then you will look for me, but I shall be no more.[65]
>
> Why is my suffering continual,
> my wound incurable, refusing to be healed?

Do you mean to be for me a deceptive stream
with inconstant waters?[66]

The Word of Yahweh has meant for me
insult, derision, all day long.
I used to say, 'I will not think about him,
I will not speak in his name any more.'
Then there seemed to be a fire burning in my heart,
imprisoned in my bones.[67]

As this prayer comes to a close, a musician takes to the stage. He sings
some songs that express a mix of both anger and passion for God.
When he has finished, someone else approaches the stage and begins
to read:

Naturally, the first priest duly appeared, and Ahab understood what
the real threat was. To compensate for it, he instituted something he
had learned from the Jews – a Day of Atonement – except that he deter-
mined to establish a ritual of his own making.

Once a year, the inhabitants shut themselves up in their houses, made
two lists, turned to face the highest mountain and then raised their
fists to the heavens.

'Here, Lord, are all the sins I have committed against you,' they said,
reading the account of all the sins they had committed. Business
swindles, adulteries, injustices, things of that sort. 'I have sinned and
beg forgiveness for having offended you so greatly.'

Then – and here lay Ahab's originality – the residents immediately
pulled their second list out of their pocket and, still facing the same
mountain, they held that one up to the skies too. And they said something like: 'And here, Lord, is a list of all your sins against me: You
made me work harder than necessary, my daughter fell ill despite all
my prayers, I was robbed when I was trying to be honest, I suffered
more than was fair.'

After reading out the second list, they ended the ritual with: 'I have
been unjust towards you and you have been unjust towards me.
However, since today is the Day of Atonement, you will forget my faults
and I will forget yours, and we will carry on together for another year.'[68]

After this has been read everyone is encouraged to use the paper and
pens on the tables to write something about which they are angry
or frustrated with God. If this is something that they wish to keep

private, they are asked to fold the paper and put an 'X' on the front. The pieces of paper are then gathered up and brought to two people who have come up to the stage. Everyone is told that after they have been read the pieces of paper will be symbolically handed over to God via a ritual of burning. Every time a piece of paper with an 'X' appears, it is burnt, unread, as a fragment of Psalm 10 is said as a prayer:

> Why standest thou far off, O Lord?
> Why hidest thou thyself in times of trouble?

As these prayers are being read out red wine is poured into the broken glasses that line the stage so that the wine spills over onto the sand. When all the prayers have been burnt there are a few moments of silence. Then one of the organizers approaches the stage with what appears to be a Bible. He opens it and begins to read:

> On judgement day a summons went forth to the sea, commanding that she give up her dead, and a voice called out to Hades that the prisoners be released from their chains.
>
> Then the angels gathered up all of humanity and brought them to the great white throne of God. All creation stood silently as a great angel opened the books.
>
> The first to be judged stood up and approached the text. As the accused looked at the charges, all humanity spoke as one:
>
> 'When we were hungry you gave us nothing to eat. When we were thirsty you gave us nothing to drink. We were strangers and you did not invite us in. We needed clothes and you did not clothe us. We were sick and in prison and you did not look after us.'
>
> Silence descended upon all of creation as the people pronounced their judgement on God.

After reading this, the organizer closes the book and begins to speak:

> We are not going to try and wrap up this evening of lament with some neat answer. Perhaps things will make sense one day, perhaps not. However, the point of this evening is not to answer for God – something only God can do. All we wish to do here is to acknowledge that in the midst of the uncertainty, we remain faithful.
>
> Part of the reason for this fragile faithfulness perhaps lies, as with Job, in the belief that our accusations will one day turn to ash in the

aftermath of God's unsearchable presence; that our legitimate concerns will one day be silenced before the one who cannot be named but who names us. For now, all we can comfort ourselves with is the possibility that the God we accuse is a God of our own creation. It is for this reason that Slavoj Žižek claims that the God we think we understand is like a Tamagotchi toy – our own creation which subsequently makes demands upon us.

As the service comes to an end a basketful of Tamagotchi toys (purchased cheaply off ebay) is handed round for people to take home.

Service 4

A/theism

---❖---

Background to the service

While most people consider Christianity as advocating theism over and against atheism, this service seeks to show that both theism and atheism are embraced within the Christian tradition. In 'A/theism' we explore how the terms 'theist' and 'atheist' can be understood as regional concepts that relate only to a specific understanding of God. This means that the term 'theism' refers to the belief in a certain understanding of God while 'atheism' refers to the rejection of a certain understanding of God. We can comprehend this when we consider how, as soon as we affirm that we believe in God, we necessarily have some understanding of what we mean by the term 'God'. Similarly, when we say that we do not believe in God, we must have an idea of what we mean by that term, for we have to have an idea of that which we are rejecting. This means that, just as one can ask a theist what God they believe in, one can ask an atheist what God they do not believe in.

Not only is Christianity atheistic insomuch as it rejects ideas of God which stand opposed to those found in its own tradition (the early Christians were called atheists because of their rejection of those deities worshipped by the Romans), but also there is a sense in which Christianity is atheistic because it rejects its own understanding of God. For a Christian who does not simultaneously reject the idea of God that he or she affirms implicitly claims that the one he or she worships can be held within his or her systems of belief.

This does not mean that Christianity teaches us to reject our religious beliefs but rather reminds us that we must engage in a process of 'de-naming' God every time we name God, acknowledging that

God's name is above every name that we could ever ascribe. One of our prime teachers in this method is Jesus himself. As we noted in Part 1, the opening words of the Lord's Prayer begin, 'Our Father in heaven, hallowed be your name'. Here God is named as 'Father', yet immediately the prayer acknowledges that this name is 'hallowed'. We are thus informed that the name is holy and set apart, thus operating in a way that is other than our culturally conditioned ideas of fatherhood. This process reminds us that God transcends all earthly names and, as such, escapes our attempts at absolute understanding. God is *nominated* and then *de-nominated*, reminding us that our understanding of the term 'Father' is profoundly affected by our background.

In opposition to the fundamentalist, who can be defined as one who believes what they believe, the Christian can be said to operate with an a/theistic discourse, which makes claims about God while simultaneously acknowledging that these claims are provisional, uncertain and insufficient. This a/theistic approach is one that understands how our questioning of God is never really a questioning of God but only a means of questioning our understanding of God. It is a discourse not unlike that of the original cynics who, in opposition to the common caricature, were deeply moral individuals who questioned truth as presented by society precisely because of their deep love of truth. An a/theistic faith thus acknowledges the importance of both theism and atheism in faith.

This approach does not stand above faith, nor does it undermine it; rather this a/theistic approach is born from, and subservient to, faith. It allows us to maintain an unflinching belief *in* God (as one believes *in* a person one trusts) while maintaining humility when attempting to describe *what* exactly God is. This is summed up powerfully by Augustine when he wrote, 'What do I love when I love my God?' – a phrase that captures a profound passion for God amidst doubt and unknowing. By exploring how fidelity to God requires an acknowledgement of the provisional nature of our beliefs, 'A/theism' was designed to offer us a greater appreciation of God's greatness, a renewed openness to learning from other people's understanding of God and a deeper commitment to a faith that is enhanced, rather than enslaved, by a particular Christian tradition.

Service description

It has been raining heavily all day and as seven o'clock approaches there is some concern that people will opt for staying at home rather than coming out to Ikon. Thankfully, it isn't long before people begin to arrive. The room itself is warm and filled with a welcoming candlelight. Attached to one of the walls are hundreds of diverse images and words, while two video projectors provide a visual backdrop that accompanies the music. Once everyone is settled the first speaker of the evening approaches the stage. Holding the microphone close, he waits for a few moments for people to finish their conversations and then begins:

> It is said that the devil used to walk late at night through different parts of the world with his friends. Once, during one of these midnight strolls, a demon who was walking with him happened to see a young woman speaking with Jesus. The demon shifted uneasily, expecting Lucifer to fly into a terrific rage, but instead he seemed unperturbed. Later the demon plucked up some courage and asked the devil why he was so unconcerned by the woman's encounter with Christ. 'Why should I care,' replied the devil, 'for in just a little while I shall make a theology of it.'[69]
>
> So many of us begin our faith with an encounter and end with nothing but a doctrine. If we could compare the journey of faith to the growth of an individual, we could say that in the childhood years we struggle to understand the mystery of God just as a child struggles to understand the mystery of the world. In response we turn to the wisdom of our religious tradition as a child turns to the wisdom of his or her parents. In our adolescence we often lose this childlike wonder, failing to realize that the wisdom passed down to us was never meant to do away with the mystery but was meant only to prevent it from being unbearable. Finally, if we ever enter into maturity, we come to experience once more that mystery for what it is.
>
> Tonight is about challenging the adolescent within us all, reminding ourselves that our images of God, important as they are, are at best icons that allow us to contemplate the mysterious presence of God, and are at worst idols which take the place of God.

As he finishes this introduction someone else comes to the mike and begins to read from a small book:

As Jesus approached Jericho, a man of great learning sat on the road-side. When he saw the crowd going by he asked what was happening. They told him, 'Jesus of Nazareth is passing by.'

In response he called out, 'Jesus, Son of David, have mercy on me!'

Those who led the way rebuked him and told him to be quiet, but he shouted all the more, 'Son of David, have mercy on me!'

Jesus stopped and ordered that the man approach. When he came near, Jesus touched him and said, 'Your faith has healed you', and at that moment he became blind. When all the people saw it they were horrified and scared. But the man left rejoicing, saying, 'I have been blinded by the most wondrous vision!'

He then closes the book and continues:

The experience of God can be compared to looking into the very centre of the sun, for when we encounter the truth we are dazzled and blinded by its white light. So much so that while the journey of becoming Christian can be described as a movement from darkness into ever more light, it can be experienced as a journey from the light of worldly wisdom into ever darker depths of God's ineffable mystery.

As the music plays, everyone is asked to reflect on the images and words that line the walls. After five minutes have passed people are asked to remove some of the images from the walls that resonate with their image of God. Then one of the speakers approaches the stage:

Many of us have lost sight of the fact that a deeply religious form of atheism lies at the heart of Christianity. This atheism is not one that rejects the idea that there is a source to the universe, nor is it simply the rejection of gods different from our own. Rather, this faith-filled atheism is one which understands that the God we worship is bigger than all our imaginings.

At the heart of fundamentalism lies a categorical rejection of this atheism, for the fundamentalist within us all resolutely affirms that our belief in God is a true reflection of what God is really like – that God is on our side. By failing to embrace this atheism, our faith becomes arrogant, narrow-minded and proud. To combat this, we must regularly remind ourselves that we are limited, finite individuals who cannot fathom the deep wells of God. We must embrace that atheism which is born, not from a lack or a rejection of faith, but rather from the heart of faith: an atheism that rejects our understanding of God precisely because it recognizes that God is bigger, better and different than we could ever imagine.

The images that you have picked from the walls symbolize some ideas that have helped you to understand God in the past. Yet regardless of how beautiful and important these images are, they do not adequately grasp our beloved. Therefore we would ask you to bring these images outside and offer them over to God, acknowledging that before the unapproachable flames of the divine, these images are but ash.

The Menagerie's fire door (which leads directly to some waste ground beside the bar) is opened. Outside it is still raining and one of those involved in the service shelters beneath an umbrella. Beside him there is a fire inside a large metal oil drum. One by one people go outside and put their paper into the fire. As they do this, the person beneath the umbrella puts his hand on their shoulder and says the following prayer:

> Lord, we offer up our images of you, acknowledging that while they are important, you stand over and above all our understanding. In love and faithfulness we offer you these fragments as we recognize the poverty of our understanding before the wealth of your presence. Amen.

When everyone has returned to the bar the fire door is closed and the service resumes. One of those who helped organize the evening shares briefly about the fears she had initially felt when helping to plan the service. She goes on to share how she overcame her concerns and embraced the act as worship rather than sacrilege. After this one of Ikon's poets offers some thoughts to the crowd before the closing liturgy is said:

Leader: Oh God, consecrate these ashes; let them be for us, not the remnants of destruction, but the refinement of our desire to know you. At present we see only confusing images in a mirror, but one day we shall see face to face. We welcome your refiner's fire; remove our wood, hay and stubble, and bless our efforts to seek after you. In Christ's name we pray.

People: Amen.

Leader: The people who walked in darkness

People: have been overwhelmed by a great light.

Leader: On those who lived in a land dark as death

People: a great light has dawned.

Leader: You have turned our laments into dancing.

People: You have stripped off our sackcloth and clothed us with joy.

Leader: You have not left us in the ashes

People: but have lifted us to a place of esteem.

Leader: And we thank you, God of all, that you do not hide your face from those who diligently seek after you. We thank you that you are not a God who dwells far away, and you did not abandon us in our death. Just as Christ is our image of God,

People: so we seek to be the image of Christ.

Leader: Send us now into the world in peace and grant us strength and courage to love and serve you with gladness and singleness of heart.

People: Amen.[70]

During this liturgy the fire outside is extinguished and the ash that has gathered at the bottom of the barrel is put into a bowl and brought inside. Once cooled, the ash is placed into small clear plastic envelopes. As the service comes to its conclusion these envelopes are given out as a reminder that, before God, all our images are but fragments.

Service 5

Advent

———◆———

Background to the service

In the last service we explored how our beliefs can so easily become a barrier that would separate us from the one whom they supposedly reveal. In this service we build upon this insight by exploring how we ought to lay aside the desire to know truth (orthodoxy as 'right belief') in favour of being a site for the transformative power of truth (orthodoxy as 'believing in the right way').

'Advent' was a Christmas gathering and thus employed the story of Mary's pregnancy as a means of understanding the manner by which this truth of God is encountered and nurtured. In an approach that parallels Mary's experience of being touched by the power of God and experiencing God growing within her womb before finally giving birth to God, this service explores how the Christian testifies to an encounter with God (as an external reality) that results in God being nourished as an internal reality which then radiates from the individual as that which transforms reality (through the individual's words and deeds).

As this service explores the central message of Christmas, namely the incarnation of the Word, we look at how this Word is incarnated in our lives as we commit to a life of openness, confession and love. As such the service was dedicated to creating an environment within which we would open ourselves up to the incoming of God, commit to nurturing the work of God in our lives and seek to enable this work to impact the lives of those around us.

Service description

It is late in December and the bar has been filled with hundreds of Christmas lights and large expanses of tinsel. At the back of the room an oversized Christmas tree sits where the pinball machine used to be. In the centre of the room there is a large table that has been covered with black material. On top sits an ornate bowl, filled with ash, and a large square of sackcloth. On one of the walls a video showing the ultra-sound scan of an unborn baby runs on a loop. At various intervals the DJ mixes the following words into the music:

> In the wilderness prepare the way for the Lord; make straight in the desert a highway for our God.[71]

As the music begins to fade someone walks to the table in the middle of the room and begins to cut away at the large piece of sack-cloth, making strips and then placing them into the bowl. As this is happening someone else approaches the stage to speak:

> At Christmas we remember the story of Mary who, one evening, was overcome by the Spirit of God. In the aftermath of this encounter she found herself nourishing the Son of God in her womb. Finally she gave birth to this child, a child who did not simply speak a message of healing but who was a message of healing.
>
> This story strikes us as amazing and unique, yet it is not to be admired from afar but rather repeated in our lives. For, just as the Spirit of God overcame Mary, so that is our longing. And just as she nurtured God in the womb of her being, so we seek to nourish God in the womb of our being. And just as Mary gave birth to the one who would trans-form the world in love, so we seek to give birth to a transforming love in the words and deeds that emanate from us.
>
> Yet, unlike Mary, we have already been impregnated with all man-ner of things, and there is little room for God. And so we seek to empty ourselves this evening, to become pure again so that we may house Christ in our thoughts and give birth to Christ in our actions.
>
> In the approach to Christmas we remember the Word becoming flesh and open ourselves up to this event occurring within our own being. And so tonight let us take time to open ourselves once more to God's glorious advent, clearing space in the womb of our being, as we seek to emulate the life of Mary in our own lives.

After this introduction some time is set aside for music and poetry. Afterwards one of the speakers approaches the front:

> Only God can give God. In order to prepare for this advent of God in our being, we must let go of those things in our lives that would extinguish the fragile flame of the Spirit. Our lives are so cluttered with the empty things of this world that there is no space for Christ. We have been impregnated by the world and the womb of our being has become a breeding place for all kinds of attachments, fears and selfishness.
>
> Meister Eckhart once said that God abhors a vacuum and speaks life into the nothing. He thus taught his disciples to empty themselves of their selfish attachments so that God would fill the gap that was created. Let us follow this example and take some time to think about the various activities we have done that should have been left undone, and the various activities we have left undone that should have been done.

After this there is some time to reflect upon our actions. After some music the speaker returns to the stage and continues:

> In order to make that space for Christ in our lives, we must commit ourselves to mending broken relationships and to living in such a way as to seek justice and mercy for those who are burdened by the greed of ourselves and our society. Only as we endeavour to die to ourselves and live by the simple way of Christ can we take part in the rest of this service. Let us take some time to reflect upon any broken relationships or injustices that must be set right in our lives before we continue.

This is followed by another brief pause for reflection. Then the speaker continues:

> In the centre of the room there is a bowl of ashes. During the service strips of sackcloth have been carefully placed into this bowl. As a sign of repentance for those things that you have been reflecting upon, we would encourage you to come forward and take a strip of sackcloth from the bowl. One of us will tie this around your wrist and then offer to say a prayer. These ashes and the strip of sackcloth are symbols of repentance that show a desire to prepare for the incoming of God. This is a symbol of our turning back to God; it is a sign of our desire for purification, of our efforts to leave aside our worldly attachments so

that the Word may again be birthed within us. As such we would encourage you to wear this sackcloth until Christmas day.

As some music plays people begin to approach the altar to receive their sackcloth. As the sackcloth is tied to each person's wrist the following prayer is said:

> This sackcloth and these ashes are a symbol of our heartfelt repentance. By wearing them we show our commitment to following the way signalled to us by Mary: a way of openness, purity and fidelity. As we approach Christmas day we would ask that you would transform those barren parts of our being into an oasis where you would dwell. Amen.

Once everyone is seated, someone stands up and reads the following parable:

> The crowd was silent, listening as Jesus prepared to tell them another story about the kingdom. Then from among the assembled people a young man in fine clothes shouted out, 'Tell us, Lord – to what can you compare the kingdom of God?'
>
> Jesus paused for a moment before looking out to sea.
>
> 'There was once a merchant,' he began, 'who spent his days searching for fine pearls. Then one day he found a priceless pearl of such beauty that he immediately went away and sold everything that he possessed so that he would have enough money to purchase it.'
>
> The crowd looked satisfied with this definition of the kingdom, especially the rich young man.
>
> 'This kingdom must be worth possessing,' he thought to himself, 'if a rich merchant would sell everything that he had in order to possess it.'
>
> Just then Jesus' attention was drawn to a young woman who was listening intently to his words. He turned from the assembled people and said to her, 'Others listen yet fail to understand, for the only sound they can hear is the beating of their own desire. You, however, have both listened and understood.'
>
> 'All I know,' replied the young woman, 'is that to sell everything to possess such a pearl would make little sense, for the owner would possess nothing but the pearl. And so, while it may be priceless, it would make the owner destitute for as long as he possessed it.'
>
> 'Yes,' Jesus replied.

'So what use, then, is this pearl?' asked the woman.

'None, if you desire it for your own selfish pursuits, for then you will find nothing but poverty. Only when it is the pearl that you desire are you rich. For then the pearl will possess you, not you the pearl.'

As the evening draws to a close the main speaker offers some concluding thoughts:

To seek out the richness of God's kingdom, one must enter a place of absolute poverty in which one lays down everything. This does not necessarily mean that we lay down all that we have, for we may do this and, having not laid down our own ego, we hold back the most important thing of all. In contrast, it may look as if someone has not laid down anything, and yet that person has laid down his or her own being, and so has given everything away. For in this latter example everything the person has is now at the disposal of God, and that individual will give, receive and lose with equal joy.

This can be illustrated in the story of an old priest who presided over a great cathedral in a once prosperous city. The kindly priest spent his days praying in the vestry and caring for the poor. As a result of his tireless work, this great building was known as a place of safety and sanctuary. A constant stream of people would approach this place seeking shelter. The priest welcomed all who came to the door and gave completely without prejudice or restraint. His hospitality was famous and his heart was known to be pure. No one could steal from this weak old man, for he considered no possession his own.

One evening in mid-winter, while the priest was praying before the cross, there was a knock on the cathedral door. The priest stood and went to the entrance. Upon opening the door he was surprised to find that there stood before him a terrifying demon with rotting flesh and dark, unyielding eyes.

'Old man,' the demon hissed, 'I have travelled many miles to seek your shelter. Will you welcome me in?'

Without hesitation the priest bid the devil welcome and beckoned him into the shelter of the church. Once across the threshold this devil spat venom onto the tiled floor and attacked the holy altar, all the while shouting blasphemy and curses.

During this time the priest knelt on the floor and continued in his devotions until it was time for him to retire for the evening.

'Old man,' cried the demon, 'where are you going?'

'I am returning home to rest, for it has been a long day,' replied the kindly priest.

'May I come with you,' said the demon, 'as I too am tired and in need of a place to eat and sleep.'

'Why yes, of course,' replied the priest, 'come, and I will prepare a meal.'

On returning to his house, the priest prepared a meal while the devil smashed the artefacts that adorned the house. He then ate the meal that was provided by the priest. Once some time had passed and the demon was fed, he turned his attention again to the priest and spoke:

'Old man, you welcomed me into your church and then into your house. I have one more request. Will you now welcome me into your soul?'

'Why of course,' said the priest. 'What I have is yours and what I am is yours.'

However, there was nothing in the old man for this devil to cling onto, no material with which to make a nest and no darkness within which to hide. All that existed in the old priest's soul was light. And so this devil turned from the priest in disgust and left, never to return.

After taking some time to tidy the house, the priest went to his room, got into bed and drifted off to sleep, all the time wondering who would visit him next.

Tonight is about preparing for the incoming of God by entering the rich place of poverty. In order to aid our personal preparations we have put together a CD to be used when you get home as part of your reflections. This CD is designed to be an aid to help you become a dwelling-place for God's Word. All we ask is that you play it from beginning to end.

Finally a CD is handed to everyone. On the front cover there is a quote from Meister Eckhart: 'It is in stillness, in the silence, that the word of God is to be heard.'[72] Unknown to the people at the time, each CD plays 45 minutes of silence.

Service 6

Judas

◆◈◆

Background to the service

This service signals a move away from the previous reflections on the mystery of God towards a series of services exploring our relations with those around us. This particular service originally took place over Easter and reflected upon the crucifixion of Jesus from the perspective of Judas. While it is a common practice to place ourselves into the biblical narrative, imagining what it would be like to be various characters, we tend to place ourselves in the position of those who love and are loved by Jesus, while placing others in the negative roles. In this service we attempt the difficult task of placing ourselves in the position of the one who betrayed Jesus with a kiss.

It is a common mistake to think that by explicitly affirming God one implicitly affirms the people of God. Indeed, much religious triumphalism is based on the idea that God is on the side of those who follow God. This led to some penetrating critiques of Christianity in the nineteenth and twentieth centuries, showing how religion can become the ultimate way of justifying one's actions on a personal or national level. Yet the idea of God being on the side of those who would claim to be the people of God has also been roundly attacked by the ancient prophets, who seemed less concerned with predicting the future than with challenging their own community for using their religious and political power to instigate an exploitative system in the name of God. In so doing they showed time and again how a genuine religious discourse must be self-critical. Luther helped reintroduce this when he commented that the Word of God arrives at our threshold as *adversarius noster* (our adversary).

This self-critique is linked directly to the repeated references concerning human sin and finitude found in the scriptures. For

115

instance, John states that 'If we claim to be without sin, we deceive ourselves and the truth is not in us',[73] while Paul writes, 'I have the desire to do what is good, but I cannot carry it out. For what I do is not the good I want to do; no, the evil I do not want to do – this I keep on doing.'[74] Without this self-lacerating element of faith, our enthronement of God can all too easily slip into an enthronement of ourselves. However, while the Christian story does legitimize a kingdom, it is clearly not the kingdom of human self-interest but rather the kingdom of love.

Indeed, Jesus' teachings continually subvert our human king-doms, and the prophets were often persecuted for their subversive wisdom that passed judgement upon the therapeutic nature of the political, religious and economic systems that their communities had constructed. The critical words of the prophets were almost always aimed squarely at their own communities, calling for internal reform, rather than at those outside their communities. Over and over we are presented with a picture of the prophet as one who would critique the very community that had nurtured him in order to call them back to their first love.

The idea that Christianity offers a means of legitimating a type of pharisaic self-righteousness crumbles in the face of this radical pro-phetic stream. Many of the criticisms of religion as self-legitimating are silenced before this subversive element within the scriptures, and speak only to those times when the Church uses its power to justify wars, condemn outsiders and legitimate its own societal position. Wherever the Church suppresses the message of Christ in favour of power, wealth and status, the prophets will always be found condemning this kingdom, claiming that it is forged by human hands in order to legitimize human endeavours. Insofar as Christianity fails to engage in self-critique, not only realizing its own conceptual limitations but also pointing out our own failings, it becomes a discourse about our kingdom and not God's.

In opposition to the perverted faith of self-legitimization, this self-lacerating faith that affirms only the kingdom and values of God, simultaneously places our own kingdom into question. Far from being something horrific, this recognition of our own limitations may well lead to a religious community more ready to embrace humility, openness and learning. As such, this service aimed to provide a space where we could reflect on and repent of times when we have betrayed our faith by doing violence to others via words, thoughts and deeds.

Service description

A projection of *The Kiss of Judas* by Giotto dominates one of the walls, while on another wall a clip of the crucifixion of Jesus from an old film is projected. The clip bears little resemblance to the original as it has been filmed off an old TV using a hand-held camera, so that the image is black and white, slightly blurred and shaking. The image has also been slowed down so that the original three-minute section takes place over an hour; this video plays throughout the service. Some old TV monitors have been placed around the room; they currently show only static. As people enter the room they are stamped with the word 'Judas' and their picture is taken with a digital camera.

The tables have been joined so as to form a single long table down the centre of the room around which everyone is to sit. In the middle of the table dozens of white candles of different sizes and shapes burn. Beside the candles there are two bottles of red wine and a bowl. The service begins with some songs from a musician. As she is playing, the two bottles of wine are poured into the bowl. The amount of wine exceeds the size of the bowl, so the wine overflows and collects in a tray beneath. When the musician finishes the people are asked to close their eyes while the following story is told as a meditation:

> It is late in the evening and you are gathered together with the other disciples in a small room for Passover. All the time you are watching Jesus while he sits quietly in the shadows listening to the idle chatter and watching the disciples' gestures.
>
> As the night progresses some bread and wine is brought to the table. It is only now that Jesus sits forward so that the shadows no longer cover his face. He slowly brings the conversation to an end by capturing each one with his intense gaze, a look that never failed to draw you in. After a moment he begins to speak:

'My friends, please take this bread, for it is my very body, broken for you.'

Every eye is now fixed on the bread that is laid on the table. While these words seem obscure, everyone picks up on their gravity.

Then Jesus pours wine into each cup.

'Take this wine and drink of it, for it is my very blood, shed for you.'

While these words make little sense, there is an ominous weight to them. Jesus continues:

'As you do this, remember me.'

Most of the gathered disciples wait for a time before eating the bread and drinking the wine, lost in their thoughts and solitude. You, however, wait even longer than the others. Indeed, you cannot bring yourself to lift your hand at all. His words had cut into your soul like a knife.

Jesus does not fail to notice your hesitation and approaches; he lifts your head with his hand so that your eyes are level with his. Your eyes only meet for a moment, but before you can turn away you are caught up in a terrifying revelation. At that instant you experience the loneliness, pain and sorrow that Jesus is carrying. You see nails being driven through skin and bone, you hear crowds jeering and the cries of pain as iron cuts against flesh. At that moment you taste the sweat that runs from Jesus like blood, and experience the suffocation, madness and pain that will soon envelop his being. More than all of this, however, you experience a trace of the separation he will feel. Nothing could prepare you for that.

In that little room, that occupies no significant space in the universe, you catch a glimpse of something that you were never meant to see. But it is unavoidable because these images are etched into his eyes. You turn to leave, to run from this place and never look back. You long for death to wrap around you. But Jesus grips you with his gaze and smiles compassionately. Then he holds you tight in his arms. He understands that the weight you now carry is so great that it would have been better if you had never been born. After some time has passed, he releases you from his embrace, lifts the wine that sits before you, and whispers,

'Take this wine, my dear friend, and drink it up, for it is my very blood and it is shed for you.'

All this makes you feel desperately uncomfortable; you shift in your chair and fumble in your pocket, all the time distracted by the silver that weighs heavy in your pouch.

As the reflection comes to a close, images of everyone in the bar (taken at the beginning of the service) begin to appear on the monitors that have been scattered around the room. The word 'Judas' has been super-imposed on the pictures so that it is faintly visible. Afterwards someone approaches the stage and begins to speak:

> At an Ikon service recently a man who was unlucky enough to have chosen to drink here on the last Sunday of the month found himself in the middle of our gathering. I guess it was a bit of a shock to go to the one place where you think you can escape religion on a Sunday, only to find that it has beaten you there. During the service he said to the person beside him, 'All these people are just insecure and afraid of life.'
>
> This prophetic insight reminded me of when Nietzsche commented that getting drunk and getting religion were pretty much the same thing – both activities of the weak, both offering an escape from the difficulties of real life with the illusion of warmth and womb-like pro-tection – prizes that come at a price, the price of clear thinking, genuine experience and worthwhile existence. And here we are: sitting in a pub, talking about God – perhaps not so strange after all.
>
> For many of us, we have been guilty of using religion as some people would use alcohol – as a means of escaping reality rather than engaging with it. Yet, by living in this way, we have blood on our hands.

At this point he dips his hands into the bowl of wine that sits on the altar.

> While facile religion can act as a justification of our actions and as a means of being comforted by the feeling that our lives are meaning-ful, genuine faith does not merely offer us such heat and light . . .

At this point the speaker picks up a burning candle.

> . . . it also burns us.

He then pours some of the wax onto his hand.

> Religion without this burning is religion without the penetrating gaze of God.

Then the candle is blown out and set down.

Genuine faith is not some weapon that shields us from the storms of life while pronouncing judgement upon others, but neither is it wholly self-destructive. Rather, it is a weapon that both shields and lacerates the one who wields it, offering comfort to the distressed and distress to the comforted. To advocate this kingdom of love, mercy and truth involves self-sacrifice and self-critique.

During the next few minutes everyone is encouraged to think of times when they have used their beliefs as a way of intellectual comfort rather than as a means of challenging their behaviour. Then everyone is asked to dip their hands in the bowl of red wine that sits on the altar and blow out one of the candles. The ritual is explained as a means of acknowledging that Christ's blood is on our hands and that we have extinguished the light of Christ in our lives.

As this is happening a musician sings 'Until the end of the World' by U2, a song that describes a conversation between Jesus and Judas. Afterwards some bowls are brought out along with two jugs of fresh water and two white towels. Before leaving everyone is encouraged to go up and let their hands be washed. As this takes place the following prayer is said:

> Lord, we acknowledge the times when we have sinned against you in thought, word and deed, and we ask that you purify our hearts as we seek to bring your love into the world. Amen.

At the end of the service a small bag is passed around the room. Inside the bag there are dozens of little badges with the word 'Judas' printed on them. Everyone is encouraged to take one of the badges. This symbolizes the pouch of coins that Judas was given when he betrayed Christ, and each badge acts as a reminder that there are times in our lives when we are like Judas.

Service 7

Prosperity

——◆——

Background to the service

Continuing our reflections on transgression, this service seeks to expose the way that religion can so often be used as a type of alchemy that seeks to use faith as a raw material from which to derive spiritual, emotional and even material wealth. We can see this inauthentic approach to faith at work when we look at some popular forms of prosperity teaching, or the fact that much evangelism is founded on the promise of heaven or the fear of hell rather than the love of Christ. Yet such self-interested faith is not always so blatant and often exists in more subtle forms.

While the modern emphasis upon the correct interpretation of doctrine is placed into serious question by those involved in the emerging conversation (as discussed in the previous section), this insight opens up a way of understanding the teaching of Christ as a way of showing us how to engage in the fluid project of interpreting correctly – that is, in a way that reads our tradition with an eye towards one's neighbour, offering love, liberation and healing to the other. Once we admit how the complexity of life, our profoundly limited horizon and the ineffable nature of God make it impossible to reduce the scriptures down to a single set of ethical principles, we are able to follow the trajectory of Jesus, who taught us to interpret our tradition in ways that bear witness to love.

In order to delve into these ideas, this service was designed as a parody of self-centred Christianity in which we believe primarily as a psychological crutch to escape reality, or in order to explain reality, at the expense of transforming reality. By beginning with a subtle parody which becomes more blatant as the service progresses, we created an environment in which people would initially countersign the content of the evening before beginning to see the consequences of that endorsement.

Service description

From the very beginning this service has a distinctly different feel from its predecessors. The room is well lit and the music is upbeat. On the stage there is a table with a bottle of champagne and a chocolate cake. Beside this table there is an armchair with a lamp beside it. A well-dressed man is sitting in the armchair reading the Bible. Once everyone has arrived, someone stands at the front of the stage and begins to speak:

> I would like to begin this month by reflecting on three experiences. First, I want to mention a conversion I had a few days ago. Second, I want to talk about a book I read a few months ago. Third, I will recall a sermon I heard a few years ago.
>
> Starting with the most recent event, a few days ago I found myself in conversation with a guy who had such a deep faith that he absolutely, totally and without equivocation believed in God. He was the perfect example of someone who suffered no doubt, uncertainty or anxiety in the face of the world. During this conversation I felt personally strengthened in my own faith and thought to myself, 'Thank you, God, that religion offers us certainty and security in a world full of ambiguity, offering us answers where there are so many questions, meaning when everything can seem so meaningless, and purpose to help us cope with our otherwise vacuous lives.' I thanked God that my faith helped me cope with the dark shadows of life, comforting me that a good God is in control rather than indifferent cosmic forces.
>
> Then there was the book I read by an author who argued that the core principle and outworking of faith was one of happiness and pleasure. And I thought to myself, 'Thank you, God, that the heart of the gospel is good news, that it lightens our heavy loads, offering a community who care for us and a belief system that fulfils us.' And I thanked God in my heart that I could love myself because I was loved.
>
> Then there was the sermon that I heard on the subject of prayer. The speaker, a well-known Christian, was reassuring us that at the core

of prayer there are three little words: 'Please help me.' And I thought to myself, 'Thank you, God, that this sermon has shown me the truth that when we are burdened and in trouble, you are at hand to help; that if we ask for a fish you will not give us a stone; that if we ask for bread you will not deliver a scorpion; that you long to bless your children and give in over-abundance; that if we have financial needs, family problems or issues at work, you will lavish upon us more than we could have imagined.'

After this the person sitting in the armchair closes his Bible and puts it down. He then turns on the lamp and begins to share his testimony. This takes place in three distinct parts with some music and poetry between each section. The first section sounds much like the beginning of any typical testimony, detailing a difficult past and the search for answers. During the first pause he gets up, cuts a piece of chocolate cake from the altar and sits back down.

The second section of his testimony builds upon the first by explaining how coming to faith helped him find new hope and a spiritual home. During the second pause he stands up, opens the champagne bottle, pours himself a glassful and takes it back to his seat.

By the third section his words are more extreme. He speaks of the happiness and security he now feels in his faith. He also describes how he gives a little money to the poor, prays at church, attends Bible studies and socializes with his Christian peers. During this time he also shares about the material and spiritual blessings that he has received from God. Having said this, he takes his cake and stuffs it greedily into his mouth, then swallows it with the aid of his champagne. He then claims that this champagne and chocolate cake is the true body and blood of Christ.

Everyone is then actively encouraged to come up to eat the chocolate cake and drink the champagne as Communion. At this point the atmosphere turns very dark. Even though people are being actively encouraged to come up to the altar, nobody moves. After a prolonged and difficult pause the following parable is read, as if from the Bible:

> Jesus withdrew privately by boat to a solitary place, but the crowds continued to follow him. Evening was now approaching and the crowds, many of whom had travelled a great distance, were growing hungry.

Seeing this, Jesus sent his disciples out to gather food, but all they could find were five loaves of bread and two fishes. Then Jesus asked that they go out again and gather up the provisions which the crowds had brought to sustain them in their travels. Once this was accomplished there stood before Jesus a mountain of fish and bread. He then directed the people to sit down on the grass.

Standing before the food and looking up to heaven, he gave thanks to God and broke the bread. Then he passed the food around his disciples and they ate like kings in full view of the starving people. But what was truly amazing, what was miraculous about this event, was that when they had finished the massive banquet there were not even enough crumbs to fill a starving hand.

In closing the following story is told:

I remember seeing a sticker that said, 'If Christianity was illegal, would there be enough evidence to convict you?' That evening I had a dream that it was true and that I was summoned before a judge.

The prosecution has quite a case against me. They begin by offering the judge dozens of photographs which show me attending church meetings, speaking at religious events and participating in various prayer and worship services. Next they offer up as evidence some of the religious books that I have been reading, followed by some of my religious CDs and trinkets. After this they step up the pace and reveal to the court many of the poems, pieces of prose and journal entries that I have written about faith. Then, in closing, the prosecution twist the bloody knife that they have skilfully used by offering my Bible to the judge. This is a well-worn book with scribbles, notes, drawings and underlining throughout – evidence, if it were needed, that I have read and re-read this sacred book.

Throughout the court case I have been sitting in fear and trembling, saturated by sweat. I know deep in my heart that, with the evidence against me, imprisonment or even death is a strong possibility. At various times throughout the proceedings I have been on the verge of standing up and denying Christ. But while this idea haunts my mind, I resist the temptation and remain focused.

Once the prosecution has finished presenting their case, the judge proceeds to ask if I have anything to add, but I remain silent and resolute, terrified that if I open my mouth, I might be weak enough to deny the charges made against me. I am then led away while the judge ponders my case.

After about an hour I am summoned back to the court-room in order to hear the verdict and receive word of my punishment. The judge enters the room, stands before me, looks deep into my eyes and states, 'Of the charges that have been brought forward I find the accused not guilty.'

'Not guilty.' My heart freezes. Then, in a split second, my fear and terror are transformed into confusion and rage. Despite myself, I stand before the judge and demand that he tell me why I am innocent of the charges, in light of all the evidence.

'What evidence?' he replies in shock.

I start by pointing out the various poems and journal entries I have written, but he simply replies that they only show that I have a way with words.

I then refer to the services I have spoken at, the worship meetings I have participated in and the conferences I have attended.

But again he simply smiles and tells me that it is only evidence that I am a public speaker and a bit of an actor who pretends to be what he is not – nothing more. And then he says that such foolishness would never be enough to convict me.

The dream ends as he looks me in the eye and says, as if informing me of a great, long-forgotten secret: 'The court is indifferent towards your Bible reading and church attendance; it has no concern for worship with words and a pen. Continue to develop your theology, and use it to paint pictures of love. We have no interest in such church-going artists who spend their time creating images of a better world. We exist for those who would lay down that brush, and their life, in a Christlike endeavour to create such a world.'

At the end of the service the remainder of the champagne and chocolate cake is handed round and people are encouraged to talk about how they felt during the service.

Service 8

Heresy

———•◆•———

Background to the service

In contrast to those who would say that God is the greatest conceivable being and those who would claim that God is utterly beyond conception, we have seen how it is pragmatically useful for the Christian to follow Anselm in the idea that God ought to be *conceived* of as that which is *greater than conception*. This means that Christianity is about being in a relationship with that which is not reducible to theoretical analysis. Indeed, Jesus spent no time that we know of engaging in deep reflections upon the nature of God, but rather revealed the outworking of God through his ministry.

While modern apologetics has championed the view that we can say substantial things about the existence and nature of God, such a view has been placed into serious question by both those outside the Church and those within it. For example, Marx, Nietzsche and Freud helped to show that any supposedly objective, scientific conception of God can easily be explained as a reflection of our cultural context, education, tradition and unconscious, while theologians such as Barth argued that to make a conceptual image of God is nothing more than forming a conceptual idol made from the materials of the human imagination. In fact we can find such thinking in the Bible itself, for in various passages we find references to God as an unnameable name (YHWH) and as an inaccessible presence that is always mediated (for no one can look upon the unmediated presence of God and live). Here God is understood to be greater than the conceptual construct 'God'; hence some people's reference to the God beyond God. 'God', rather than being a straightforward concept, is thus a term that stands in the place of the one whom we love but cannot grasp.

This does not rule out the possibility of divine revelation but simply acknowledges that our finite, fragile minds cannot fully understand it, for any revelation will inevitably be affected by our biological limitations, cultural prejudices and upbringing. We can thus think of God's revelation as a secret that remains secret in its telling, for while a normal secret is no longer a secret when it is shared, God's revelation, by remaining inaccessible in its telling, remains secret in the sharing. Here mystery and revelation are brought together in an irreducible tension.

By drawing people's attention to the limits of our understanding, this service explores how, before God, we are all heretics. Far from being something to reject, mourn over or attempt to overcome, we show how such a recognition can be deeply liberating. Indeed, the heart of this service involves a form of repentance over times in our lives when we have suppressed this insight and have become dogmatic and violent in our beliefs.

Service description

The tables that usually sit in the centre of the bar have been cleared to make room for a large makeshift cross that lies flat across the room. As people enter they are asked to sign their name on this cross using some black markers that have been left to one side. Spread around the room are various mirrors, some of which have the word 'heretic' scrawled across them. Once everyone has signed their name, the music begins to fade and someone comes to the front to speak:

Recently a well-respected church leader attended one of our gatherings in order to witness first hand what took place. Afterwards he leaned over to someone at the bar and said, 'This has been interesting, but is it Christian?'

When I heard this I was genuinely amazed that someone with his insight and wisdom could have expressed such uncertainty. Is this community Christian? Surely the answer was obvious . . . of course not.

If Christianity is about expressing a service to Christ, if it means radiating divine love in a broken world or sacrificing oneself selflessly in response to the needs of the other, then this community is nothing more than a fragile group of people struggling to become Christian. This sacred/secret place represents the place within which we openly acknowledge that we are the ones who need to be evangelized. Here we acknowledge our brokenness, frailty and heresy.

After this brief introduction someone approaches the stage and begins to speak:

Christian tradition holds that the apostle Peter, late in his life, travelled to Rome to become that city's first bishop to its Christian community, and that he was martyred under the persecutions by the emperor Nero around 64 AD. Tradition also holds that Peter was sentenced to crucifixion, and upon hearing his fate, was aghast, protesting his unworthiness to die in the same manner as his lord, saviour and friend, Jesus.

What went through the mind of Peter in these moments? Did he think back to another time, almost seemingly to another life, when he denied even knowing Jesus?

Or perhaps he didn't think of this past moment of weakness and fear; maybe he thought of some other split second of weakness, in the face of persecution . . .

Had he actually denied Christ again and, like Christ, been betrayed?

The apocryphal *Acts of Peter* tells us that Peter, fleeing from persecution in Rome, met Christ on the road and asked him, 'Lord, where are you going?' Christ answered, 'I am going to be crucified again,' and Peter, struck to the heart, turned around to go back and meet his martyrdom.

Did the guards and soldiers mock this weeping, lunatic old Jew, mumbling something about being unworthy of crucifixion? In response to this, Peter was crucified upside down. And for this reason, the inverted cross, the cross of St Peter, became one of the earliest Christian symbols.

It is a symbol of devotion to Christ in the face of weakness, of humility and self-examination.

It is the cross that freely admits that we now see only confusing images in a mirror, but we look forward to the time when we will see face to face.

It is the cross of a foul-mouthed fisherman who became a bishop.

For us today, it is the cross that says, 'I am not God.' 'I am no Christ.'[75]

As this is being said, the cross that lies across the floor is slowly lifted until it rests against the wall. It is lifted so that, when upright, it forms the St Peter's cross.

Everyone is then asked to reflect upon this as our cross, as that which recognizes our humanity and limitations. After a few minutes everyone is encouraged to come up and kneel before or embrace this upside down cross. Once everyone who wishes to do so has come up, the following parable is read, as if from a Bible:

> At dawn he appeared again in the temple courts, where all the people were gathered around him, and he sat down to teach.
>
> At that moment we, the teachers of the law and the Pharisees, brought in a woman caught in the sin of heresy.
>
> We humiliated her by making her stand before the group, then we turned to Jesus and said,
>
> 'Great teacher, this woman was caught perverting the law, spreading false witness and tainting the name of our God. Our law demands that we stone anyone who would so spoil the image of God. Now what do you say?'
>
> We were using this question as a trap, in order to have a base for accusing him.
>
> But Jesus remained silent. Instead of answering us he bent down and started to write on the ground with his finger.
>
> In the sand he inscribed the names of every person in this room.
>
> When we kept on questioning him, he straightened up and said, 'If any of you have not perverted the law of God, if any among you has not spoken falsely of heavenly things nor muddied the divine image with hasty words and deeds, then you may be the first to cast a stone.'
>
> Again he stooped down and wrote on the ground.
>
> Under each of our names he began to carve out the sins and secrets that lay deep in our hearts.
>
> While Jesus wrote, we who were present began to leave, one at a time, the older ones first, until only Jesus and the woman were left.
>
> After a time Jesus slowly straightened up, looked the woman compassionately in the eyes and tenderly asked her, 'Woman, where are they now? Has no one condemned you?'
>
> 'No one, sir,' she replied.
>
> 'Then neither do I,' Jesus declared.

After some music and discussion the service closes with the following meditation:

> It is late in the evening and you are huddled quietly around a campfire with dozens of other disciples, listening intently to Jesus as

he tells stories of heaven. For many hours he has spoken eloquently about a land full of great mansions, a world with streets of gold and vast expanses of fertile land.

By the time Jesus has finished, it is approaching dawn and the fire is burning out. While everyone else has drifted off to sleep with the images of treasure and mansions dancing in their minds, you remain awake.

Soon only you and Jesus are left to watch over the dying fire.

After a little time has passed you turn to Jesus and speak:

'My Lord, each day more people come to worship you. Every day I am surrounded by large numbers of disciples with great learning and courage who have sacrificed everything for you and your message. I can't help wondering whether someone like me, a self-centred, self-interested sinner, will be overlooked amidst all the great thinkers, politicians, preachers and radicals who are being attracted to you and your message.'

After a few moments you continue:

'I've never lived in a mansion; in fact I have never even been inside one. So I don't care much if I miss out. But tell me, will there be a place for me when I die?'

Jesus looks at you with compassion:

'Fear not,' he whispers, in a tone that could barely be heard over the content noises of the sleeping crowd. 'Tucked away in a corner of heaven, far from all the mansions and streets of gold, there is a little stable. It is cramped and old, but on a clear night you can see the stars amidst the cracks and feel the warm air on your flesh. It is there that I will dwell, and while it may be no mansion, there is a space in that place for you.'

As the service comes to an end, a bagful of little St Peter's crosses is passed around. Each person takes and keeps a cross.

Service 9

Corpus Christi

Background to the service

In Part 1 we explored how the Christian narrative opens up a different understanding of truth from that which is found in the Western world. Instead of truth being seen as a series of propositions that *correspond* to the way the world actually is, we find the idea of truth as that which *transforms* the way the world actually is. To have the truth as spoken of by Christ does not mean that we can somehow know God in an epistemological way, but rather that we are in relationship with God and outworking that relationship in the world.

In contrast to the idea that one can know God by the study of systematic theology, Jesus introduced the idea that one could know God by finding God in the other. The idea of loving others as the sign of knowing God (1 John 4.16) complements the idea that in loving others we come face to face with God in the face of the other (Matthew 25.40). This radical commitment to those around us results from a genuine love that is born from God, emanates from God, testifies to God and encounters God.

The focus of faith thus changes from the modern emphasis upon 'right belief' (orthodoxy) and 'right practice' (orthopraxis) to an emphasis upon believing in the right way and practising in the right way. In other words, in the absence of absolute knowledge, we must seek to live and believe in a way that offers healing, liberation and love to the world, all the while acknowledging that the manner of doing this cannot be worked out fully in advance.

In contrast to the modern emphasis upon *what* we believe, we must learn again how the test of faith is, from beginning to end, evidenced in *how* we believe – that is, in how our beliefs challenge, transform and liberate the existence of others and ourselves. In short, how do our beliefs help to transform us into the image of Christ? In 'Corpus Christi' we attempt to explore the idea of a faith which is concretely immersed in the world and which consequently recognizes and celebrates the importance of flesh.

This service thus seeks to celebrate this sensual element of Christianity via a celebration of physicality. Out of this celebration the service offers a challenge to embrace the message of love.

Service description

As people enter the room they are greeted by bowls filled with fruit on various tables and images of the human body projected onto one of the walls. At the front of the room there is a table full of various fruits with a chopping-board and knife. The DJ plays for around ten minutes while people order a drink and chat. At the back of the room a figure stands with a mike. At around a quarter past seven this person begins with a story:

> Early one morning a young man knocked on the door of his beloved. Moments later he heard her say, 'Who is it?'
>
> 'It is I,' he replied.
>
> But the door remained shut and his beloved simply said, 'Then please leave this place, for there is not enough room in my house for two.'
>
> Saddened, the lover left that place.

After a few minutes of music someone comes to the stage and speaks:

> There was once a young and gifted woman who set herself the almost impossible task of setting up a printing press so that she could translate and distribute the Word of God to the people. Yet such a job would require a great deal of money, and so, almost as soon as she had conceived the idea, she sold the few items that she possessed and went to live on the streets, begging for the money that she needed.
>
> Raising the necessary funds took many years, for while there were a few who gave generously, most only gave a little, if anything at all. But gradually the money began to accumulate.
>
> However, shortly before the plans for the printing press could be set in motion, a dreadful flood devastated a nearby town, destroying

many people's homes and livelihoods. Without hesitation the woman used all the money she had gathered to feed the hungry and rebuild lost homes.

Once the town began to recover, the woman silently went back to the streets in order to start all over again, collecting the money needed to translate the Word of God.

Many more years passed, with many cold winters that caused great suffering to the woman. Then, shortly before the target amount was reached, disaster struck again. This time a deadly plague descended like a cloud over the city, stealing the lives of thousands.

By now the woman was herself tired and ill, yet without thought she spent the money she had collected on medicines and care for the sick and orphaned.

Then, once the shadow of the plague lifted, she again went onto the streets, driven by her desire to translate the Word of God.

Finally, shortly before her death, this faithful woman gathered the money needed for the printing press and completed the project she had set herself many years before.

After she had passed away, it is rumoured by some that this godly woman had actually spent her time making three translations of the Word, the first two being the most splendid of all.[76]

Tonight is a celebration of the body, a celebration of our body and the body of the other. It is also an exploration of the idea that we are the body of Christ and that Christ is to be found in the body of our neighbour, whoever they turn out to be. Tonight we wish to reflect upon how to offer our bodies to one another as Christ offers his body for us.

After this opening there is some time for music, poetry and discussion on the theme of love and sacrifice. After this the person at the back of the room speaks again:

The young lover didn't know quite what to do. He went for a long walk before deciding to call again at the house of his beloved. By the time he returned it was early in the afternoon. Again he knocked and once more he heard her say, 'Who is it?'

'It is I,' he responded, hoping that he would find her in better form.

But once more she responded by saying, 'Then please leave this place, for there is not enough room in my house for two.'

Once more he turned and left.

As this is being said, some of the fruit on the table at the front of the room is cut into pieces and placed on plates. After the reflections people are invited to approach the table and take some segments of fruit. Once everyone has some fruit they are encouraged to offer it to another in the room while saying, 'This is a symbol of my body, broken for you.'

After this the person at the back of the room speaks again:

> Upon leaving his beloved's house he called in on some friends for advice, for by this stage he was very worried. His friends suggested that he leave her alone until after tea and then return again with some flowers. And so he went and bought some roses and waited until early in the evening. When he finally got to her door, he held his breath and knocked again.
>
> 'Who is it this time?' came the response.
>
> 'It is I. Please let me in,' he responded.
>
> 'I have already told you twice that there is no room for two in this place,' she replied. 'Now please go and leave me alone.'
>
> Once more he turned to leave.

This is followed by a musician who plays 'Wonderful disguise' by Mike Scott (a song based on a quote by Mother Teresa about people being a disguise of God). Afterwards someone comes up to the stage and addresses those who have gathered:

> On 25 September 1941, after all the Jews of Eiskysky and the nearby towns had been rounded up, the 4,000 captives were led to the horse market. In groups of 250 they were taken to the old Jewish cemetery and ordered to undress in front of a line of open ditches. (All this was done under the watch and encouragement of local people.)
>
> The leader of the executions, Ostrovakas, dressed in a white apron and gloves, personally supervised the killing, reserving the right to murder the town's leaders and practise sharp-shooting on the children.
>
> On that dark day Michalowsky and his 16-year-old son Zvi stood shivering before the open graves. Zvi spent those moments counting the bullets and the amount of time that elapsed between each volley of fire. This meant that a split second before the shots ripped into him, he was able to go limp and fall into the ditch.
>
> He waited for what seemed an eternity as more bodies piled on top of him. He struggled to breathe among the corpses, gagging on the river of blood and the smell of dead flesh.

Very early on 26 September, in the dead of night, he struggled from the grave, all the time listening to the festivities that were still going on in the distance. It seemed that most of the village was out singing, laughing and rejoicing at the massacre.

At the far end of the cemetery, near a huge church, Zvi knew of some Christian families and so he approached them, still naked and covered in blood.

He knocked on the first door. After a few moments the door opened and a peasant woman whom he knew, holding a lamp, looked out. Zvi recognized that the lamp was Jewish and had been pillaged from the empty homes of his community. He pleaded with the woman, saying, 'Please let me in.' But she only shook her fist and said, 'Go back to the grave where you belong, Jew.'

Zvi tried some other houses but the response was the same.

Finally he decided to visit a Christian widow, who lived at the edge of the village near a forest. The old woman answered the door to Zvi holding a small piece of burning wood. 'Please let me in,' he begged, but the woman raised the stick and waved it at him wildly, as if warding away a demon, saying, 'You belong in the cemetery, Jew.'

But Zvi stood firm and replied, 'Do you not recognize me? I am your Lord and Saviour Jesus Christ. I have come down from the cross to visit you. Look at my blood, my suffering, my innocence. Do not disown me.'

The widow dropped onto her knees and crossed herself before kissing his blood-stained feet. All she could say was 'My God, my God,' as she led him into the house.

He stayed there for three days and three nights before finally setting out. He made her promise to tell no one about his visit, not even the priest. Before he left she provided him with warm food, fresh clothes and cold water for the journey.

Zvi survived and began the Jewish partisan movement in the vicinity of Eiskysky.[77]

While Zvi lied in order to survive, in lying he told the most profound truth of all. For in Zvi, the Messiah did visit that woman.

In closing, the person at the back of the room finishes his story:

By now it is very late and the lover has spent many hours in contemplation. Finally he throws the flowers away and decides to visit his beloved's house one last time. When he arrives he knocks on the door and hears her say, 'Who is it?'

But this time he responds by saying, 'It is not I, for we are one. There is no I but thou.'

After a brief pause the door swings open and his beloved responds by saying, 'And likewise, there is no I but thou.'

To this day they live together in that little house built for one.[78]

As the service ends, the remainder of the fruit is given out for people to eat, as they reflect on the content of the evening.

Service 10

Queer

Background to the service

To conclude, I have chosen to outline a service that deals with a subject that many will think to be divisive – namely, that of sexual orientation. However, it is not my desire to finish with something divisive at all; rather, I wish to end Part 2 with a service that has the potential of bringing a deep unity. While what follows may seem to be about sexuality, in a deeper way it is a service utterly dedicated to the subject of love.

It is worth pointing out once more that Ikon represents neither a conservative nor a liberal perspective. One way to think of Ikon relates to the idea of a doughnut. Just as a doughnut has no interior, but is made up entirely of an exterior, so Ikon has no substantial doctrinal centre. At Ikon we do not tithe to the 'organization', nor do we look to it for pastoral support. Rather, Ikon encourages relational tithing and relational pastoring whereby we give to one another materially and emotionally. Even those of us who help to set up and run Ikon events would not see ourselves as central to Ikon, and often get defensive if we are thought to fully endorse what takes place under the Ikon banner. This does not mean that there is no leadership, but rather that the role of the leadership team is to help support, serve and develop the relationships that organically arise from the group.

While Ikon, as an abstract idea, is neither liberal nor conservative, these perspectives are each represented in the actual beliefs of the various people who attend. One of the ways that we find unity amidst such diversity is via our rejection of what we can call the temptations of consumption and repulsion. Consumption and repulsion represent two ways in which we commonly engage with those who disagree with us. The first connotes the act of eating and relates to a way of engaging with someone that seeks to make them into part of our own community (just as eating an animal makes it a part of our own biological structure). Here we attempt to compel the other to think and act as we do. This is not a form of persuading the other, as in a dialogue, but rather of defeating the other, as in a battle. Repulsion represents the other side of this coin, by which we utterly reject that which is different and treat it like an enemy. Here we scapegoat that which is different and exclude it from our community.

In order to find an alternative way of relating to each other that does not fall into either revulsion or consumption, Ikon engages in two complementary approaches that can be articulated in relation to the area of sexual orientation. The first concerns the creation of a space in which genuine discussion and heartfelt disagreement concerning the issues can take place. In the run-up to this particular service we took time in both 'The Last Supper' and 'Minikon'[79] to discuss these issues in depth. However, along with these discussions we were also committed to creating a space in which we are able to challenge the way in which we hold the views which we hold. While this second approach is represented in the service below it is worth remembering that this was part of a wider context of mature debate and discussion.

In what is represented below the challenge is to consider our attitudes to those whom we disagree with. For just as those of us who reject the idea that a diversity of sexual orientations can be encompassed within Christianity have often excluded or attempted to forcibly convert those who believe that Christianity can embrace a diversity of sexual orientations, so the violence has often worked the other way around. This service was an attempt to challenge us *all* about our views while also affirming Ikon as a safe space for those of us who are gay. The use of the term 'us' in this context is very important, for in Ikon all who are a part of the community, whether gay or straight, theist or atheist, liberal or conservative (and of course all who fall between these binaries), are embraced as part of the community. When speaking of these issues, we avoid the use of the word 'you' to describe someone with a different view or set of desires.

By creating a space for in-depth discussion alongside a space in which we can set aside these discussions in order to affirm one another, Ikon seeks to short-circuit the revulsion/consumption binary in favour of loving dialogue.

Service description

As people enter the bar, their eyes are immediately drawn to a stage that has been constructed in the centre of the room. On this stage there is a bare-chested man standing motionless. A young woman is circling him with a brush and black paint. She is writing words such as 'gay', 'queer', 'homosexual', 'faggot' and 'sodomite' on his flesh as he stands there passively. Dozens of large rocks have been scattered around the floor. As the DJ plays, people order their drinks and take their seats. There is very little conversation in the room; most people seem transfixed by the young man and woman in the centre of the room. After about ten minutes have passed, the music fades and someone approaches the front to speak:

> There are those of us who would like Ikon to be a liberal Christian voice in Northern Ireland, offering a genuine alternative to the dominant conservative voice. And there are those of us who see Ikon as a revitalizing force that reimagines and reinforces the traditional religious institutions. But Ikon is neither of these.
>
> Why? Because in Ikon we are unified, not on the level of some specific set of doctrines, but rather in our desire that our beliefs, whatever they are, help to enable us to be more open to the divine and more open to one another, exhibiting a loving, caring and Christ like way of being in the world.
>
> At the door of The Menagerie we do not take off our shoes, but as we enter that door we do attempt to lay aside our differing ideologies, vital as these are, so that we may better understand one another.
>
> We need our beliefs, for they help to inform us about who we are and how we ought to live, and there are plenty of places within Ikon to discuss such things – but not here. During this sacred hour we seek only to be Christ to the other and to find Christ in the other.
>
> For this hour we lay down our interest in the current religious debates that are going on all around us. Those who would like us to make a strong statement concerning the subject will be disappointed; even those who wish us to say that we are undecided on the issue will be let down.

Here, in this sacred space, the only issue concerns how we love and embrace one another.

In the same way that this place is equally for those of us who are more theologically conservative and those of us who are more theologically liberal, as well as for those of us who believe in God and those of us who do not, so Ikon is equally for those of us who are straight and those of us who are gay.

The wider debates and discussions concerning all these things can and must happen, for we are not advocating some secular space which would illegitimately claim that all such beliefs are purely private matters. But in this room, for the next hour, we lay down these debates to concentrate on the fact that all are welcome at the table and to reaffirm that the only ones who are excluded are those who exclude themselves by not wanting to sit with others, listen to others, learn from others and love others. We are a community attempting to work out what it means to be open to God, to loving and to being transformed in love, and as such, the community is primarily for those who embrace this journey – whether conservative or liberal, protestant or catholic, theist or atheist, gay or straight. This is the unity that exists amidst our diversity – and this is why we need this place.

The next 20 minutes are taken up by the reading of three anonymous stories written by participants in the Ikon community who are gay. These stories reflect some of the difficulties these people have faced with regard to their sexual identity. After this the following story is told:

It was one of the watershed events in my life, like your first car, your first day at university, or when you decided to like coffee or dislike Madonna. They were the decisions that, one way or another, started to define your life and your identity. For me, of course, the one that truly stands head and shoulders above all those mundanities was the day that I finally decided to inform my parents that I was straight.

It seemed so absurd not to tell them. I was an adult; I'd moved out years ago. Everyone close to me knew I was straight. And my sister swore up and down that my father had known for years.

I don't know what exactly I was expecting, but what I got was that reserved and quiet resignation and forced understanding which seems to be unique to people of my parents' generation. My mother, who has always disliked the term 'straight', kept using the word 'heterosexual', which made me feel a bit like a lab animal.

My father didn't let on whether he'd known or not, but his composed exterior did seem reasonably genuine. As with most other things, he was processing it all deep inside himself: 'My son is a straight man. My son is attracted to women.' We've always got on fine, and I do think that he didn't want to turn into the stereotypical disappointed dad.

Introducing them to Elizabeth was the next hurdle. This, of course, was like having to do the whole announcement all over again. This was when it all became real. I was inviting my parents into my whole 'heterosexual' world. Luckily, Liz is incredible, and once they'd met her, my parents enjoyed her very much as a person. After they'd left, Liz and I had a good laugh at my mother's studied usage of the word 'heterosexual'.

I should have known that the final hurdle would be big family get-togethers like Christmas. My mother has quietly made it known to me that she'd 'prefer' that Liz not come, the pretence being not upsetting my grandmother. It's not the first time that my mother has pulled this tactic out of the bag, by the way – make my grandma the villain. I just wanted to scream, 'Grandma *knows*!' She's known I was straight since I was 14! Never have I felt more accepted by anyone on earth than by her, and she's 85! Why do you think that I talk to her, Mother, and not to you? It's because *she* was the one who looked deep into a teenager's eyes and said, 'Well, don't you *ever* forget that God loves you, and *I* love you . . . Now go out there and meet some gorgeous girl!'

Thanks, grandma.[80]

After some music and a time for reflection, someone comes to the stage and explains the evening's ritual:

The stones that have been scattered around the room represent our various judgements. The problem is not that we have judgements but rather that these judgements can often be destructive. As such, we have provided sheets of bubble-wrap, located around the centre stage. This is an opportunity for those of us whose beliefs, whether liberal or conservative, have done violence, to repent by wrapping one of these rocks in the bubble-wrap that is located at the centre stage. By wrapping the stones we are saying that while our beliefs are important, we do not wish these perspectives to do violence to those around us.

People are then encouraged to come up and wrap a stone with the bubble-wrap, tying it with a piece of string. This ritual is followed by the following story:

> There is an ancient legend that speaks of the gods' failed attempt to guide humanity. The deities had grown tired of the way that mortals constantly lost their way, creating any number of disasters as they interacted with one another. And so they sent out their couriers to gather together all the great, eternal wisdom that was contained in the world and refine it into a mammoth library, a library which mortals could use in order to work out how they should live and act.
>
> When the great task was completed, the colossal library stood proudly in one of the world's great cultural capitals. However, it contained too many books for any individual to read, and the library's sheer size was enough to put people off even entering. So the gods demanded that their couriers compress the wisdom into a single, encyclopaedic book.
>
> Once completed, the work was widely circulated, but the text was so huge that one could hardly lift it, let alone read and apply it. Once more the gods put their couriers to work, crafting a booklet with all the essential information, but the people were lazy and there were many who could not even read, so the booklet was refined into a single word, and the word was sent out on the lips of a messenger.
>
> And the word?
>
> It was 'love'.

In closing, the following poem is read; a copy of the poem is simultaneously projected onto the wall for people to speak aloud as a liturgy if they wish:

In the Way Things Have Been
We have said:
we are gay
we are straight
we are queer
we are not
we are men
we are women
we have divided our own Body into Us and Them.
We have believed lies
we have told lies.

And the Way Things Could Be:
Our God calls us to believe that
all men, all women, are human
equal in the sight of eternity.
We share the same breath
we inhabit our bodies
we are all fed by blood
and love
and food
and water.
We celebrate and mourn
we rejoice and we grieve.

We Search for a New Way of Being:
We have been created with dignity
we have been created in love.
We respond to the call to return to who we truly are
who we were meant to be
in Community, in Diversity, in Conversation, in Love.
We are the Body of Christ.
The Body of Christ is queer,
is man, is woman,
is straight.
The Body of Christ is the people of God,
gathered here, and carried in our hearts.
This is the body we have, this is our body.[81]

At the end people are encouraged to take their rocks away and use them as an aid for personal reflection in the coming week.

Notes

Introduction

1 Ludwig Wittgenstein, *Tractatus Logico-Philosophicus*, trans. D. F. Pears and B. F. McGuinness (London, Routledge, 2001), p. 89. These words were subsequently taken on by those who pioneered the growth of positivism and humanism in the latter half of the twentieth century.

2 It should be said that my approach to mysticism has been influenced by critiques explored in the philosophy of people such as Kant, Nietzsche, Marx, Levinas and Derrida. While such an exploration lies outside the remit of this book, I ought to mention that I do not uncritically follow all the tenets of a traditionally mystical approach, but rather believe that it is deepened and developed in dialogue with the above thinkers. I will deal with these issues elsewhere.

3 G. K. Chesterton, *Orthodoxy* (London, Fontana Books, 1908), p. 9.

Part 1: Heretical Orthodoxy

1 God rid me of God

4 The term 'science' is important precisely because every science has an object of study (for example, biology studies organic systems, chemistry looks at chemical compounds and physics explores the basic building-blocks of the universe), and for traditional theology the object is God. Of course, this 'object' of study is not one object among others but is rather a unique object, and for this reason theology was often called the 'queen of sciences'.

5 The Enlightenment period, or the Age of Reason, dates from around the seventeenth century in England, and spread into France and Germany throughout the eighteenth century before falling into disrepute in the nineteenth century. It represented a rejection of the scholastic philosophy of the middle ages, which was perceived as superstitious and authoritarian, in favour of reason. The Enlightenment thinkers argued that beliefs must be accepted or rejected on the basis

147

of reason rather than custom, authority or instinct. It was at this time, with people such as Francis Bacon, that the idea of science as a discipline – by which an hypothesis is formed, experiments are undertaken, inductive generalizations are made and tests are carried out for the purpose of verification and/or falsification – gained acceptance.

6 The term 'singular' is important because there was a belief that there was one true interpretation of what was given, be that the one meaning of the scripture verse or the one true way of understanding biological processes.

7 This has been called the 'genealogical critique', as it sought to chart the various factors that helped to birth an idea, thus undermining the belief that our ideas derive from pure reason devoid of prejudice.

8 I am indebted to Philip Harrison's unpublished essay, 'A whisper will be heard' for these insights.

9 Exodus 32.1.

10 Exodus 32.4.

11 Exodus 32.5.

12 Exodus 20.21.

13 See Isaiah 45.15.

14 Isaiah 30.20.

15 Exodus 20.4–5.

16 Exodus 33.21–23.

17 Judges 6.22; 13.22.

18 1 Kings 19.13.

19 Isaiah 6.1–5.

20 See Exodus 34.13; Deuteronomy 7.5; 16.22; 2 Kings 3.2; 10.26–27; 11.18.

21 For instance, see Exodus 16.10; Numbers 12.5; Psalms 99.7; 104.3.

22 Isaiah 19.1.

23 Slavoj Žižek explores this in *The Puppet and the Dwarf* (London, MIT Press, 2003), p. 125.

24 See Romans 8.18.

25 John 1.18; 4.12.

26 1 Timothy 6.15–16.

27 2 Corinthians 12.4.

28 Romans 11.

29 Colossians 2.8.

30 John 5.37.

31 2 Corinthians 5.7.

32 *Meister Eckhart*, ed. and trans. Raymond B. Blakney (New York, HarperPerennial, 1941), p. 231.

2 The aftermath of theology

33 See Paul Ricoeur, 'Experience and Language in Religious Discourse', in Dominique Janicaud et al., eds., *Phenomenology and the Theological Turn* (New York, Fordham University Press, 2000), pp. 127–8.
34 See Gregory of Nyssa, *The Life of Moses*, trans. Everett Ferguson and Abraham Malherbe (New York, Paulist Press, 1978), pp. 94–5.
35 Quoted in Richard Woods, *Mysticism and Prophecy* (London, Darton, Longman and Todd, 1998), p. 53.
36 Augustine, *De Doctrina Christiana*, trans. R. P. H. Green (London, Clarendon Press, 1996).
37 Dionysius the Areopagite, *Mystical Theology and the Celestial Hierarchies*, trans. Editors of The Shrine of Wisdom (Surrey, The Shrine of Wisdom, 1965), p. 10.
38 Dionysius the Areopagite, *Mystical Theology and the Celestial Hierarchies*, p. 9.
39 St Anselm, *Monologion and Proslogion*, trans. Thomas Williams (Cambridge, Hackett Publishing Company, 1996), p. 109.
40 St Anselm, *Monologion and Proslogion*, p. 109.
41 Quoted in Daniel Clendenn, *Eastern Orthodox Christianity* (Michigan, Baker, 1997), p. 57.
42 1 Timothy 6.16.
43 St Anselm, *Monologion and Proslogion*, p. 99.
44 Jean-Luc Marion, 'Is the Ontological Argument Ontological?' in Ilse N. Bulhof and Laurens ten Kate, eds., *Flight of the Gods* (New York, Fordham University Press, 2000), p. 87.
45 See James Elkins, *On the Strange Place of Religion in Contemporary Art* (London, Routledge, 2004), p. 107.
46 The word 'epistemology' refers to the area of philosophical discourse which explores the area of knowledge acquisition.

3 A/theology as icon

47 In response to this, some claim that we are led into a relativistic space in which all interpretations have equal value. This is the subject of Chapter 5.
48 In Philippians 2.9 we read that Jesus was given the 'name above every name'.
49 1 Corinthians 2.1–5.
50 Jean-Luc Marion, *God Without Being*, trans. Thomas A. Carlson (London, University of Chicago Press, 1991), p. 107.

51 Quoted in Michael Cox, *Christian Mysticism* (London, Aquarian Press, 1986), p. 78.

4 Inhabiting the God-shaped hole

52 Quoted from Alan Jacobs, *A Theology of Reading* (Oxford, Westview Press, 2001), p. 43.
53 Albert Camus, *The Outsider*, trans. Joseph Laredo (London, Penguin Books, 1982), p. 111.
54 Blaise Pascal, *Pensées*, trans. W. F. Trotter (London, J. M. Dent & Sons, 1947), p. 58.

5 The third mile

55 1 John 4.7–16.
56 Exodus 1.15–20, italics mine.
57 John 7. 6–10. The word 'yet' in the sentence, 'I am not yet going up to the feast' are not found in early manuscripts.
58 Adapted from Anthony DeMello, *The Song of the Bird* (London, Image Books, 1981), p. 48.
59 DeMello, *The Song of the Bird*, pp. 45–6.
60 Matthew 5.41.
61 *Meister Eckhart*, ed. and trans. Raymond B. Blakney (New York, HarperPerennial, 1941), pp. 33–4.

Part 2: Towards Orthopraxis

1 'Eloi, Eloi, lama sabachthani?'

62 Written by Jon Hatch.

2 Prodigal

63 Blaise Pascal, *Pensées*, trans. W. F. Trotter (London, J. M. Dent & Sons, 1947), p. 58.

3 Sins of the Father

64 Adapted from Zvi Kolitz, *Yosl Rakover Talks to God* (London, Jonathan Cape, 1999).

65 Job 7.12ff.
66 Jeremiah 15.18.
67 Jeremiah 20.8.
68 Quoted from Paulo Coelho, *The Devil and Miss Prym* (London, HarperCollins, 2000), pp. 122–4.

4 A/theism

69 Adapted from a story quoted in Anthony DeMello, *The Song of the Bird* (London, Doubleday, 1981), p. 39.
70 Adapted from a liturgy written by Jon Hatch.

5 Advent

71 Isaiah 40.3.
72 *Meister Eckhart*, ed. and trans. Raymond B. Blakney (New York, HarperPerennial, 1941), p. 107.

6 Judas

73 1 John 1.8.
74 Romans 7.18–19.

8 Heresy

75 Written by Jon Hatch.

9 Corpus Christi

76 Adapted from a Buddhist parable.
77 Yaffa Eliach, *Hasidic Tales of the Holocaust* (New York, Oxford University Press, 1982), pp. 53–5.
78 Adapted from Anthony DeMello, *The Song of the Bird* (London, Image Books, 1981), pp. 99–100.

10 Queer

79 'The Last Supper' is an event in which twelve people gather together once a month with an invited guest. Over some food and wine we

then discuss an issue related to the beliefs of the individual we have invited. It is also playfully called 'The Last Supper' to tell the guest that if they do not prove convincing this may well turn out to be their last supper. 'Minikon' is a regular meeting in which we discuss the issues raised at the main gathering in more depth.

80 Written by Jon Hatch.
81 Written by Pádraig Twomey.

About Paraclete Press

Who We Are

Paraclete Press is an ecumenical publisher of books and recordings on Christian spirituality. Our publishing represents a full expression of Christian belief and practice—from Catholic to Evangelical, from Protestant to Orthodox.

Paraclete Press is the publishing arm of the Community of Jesus, an ecumenical monastic community in the Benedictine tradition. As such, we are uniquely positioned in the marketplace without connection to a large corporation and with informal relationships to many branches and denominations of faith.

We like it best when people buy our books from booksellers, our partners in successfully reaching as wide an audience as possible.

What We Are Doing

Books

Paraclete Press publishes books that show the richness and depth of what it means to be Christian. Although Benedictine spirituality is at the heart of all that we do, we publish books that reflect the Christian experience across many cultures, time periods, and houses of worship.

We publish books that nourish the vibrant life of the church and its people—books about spiritual practice, formation, history, ideas, and customs.

We have several different series of books within Paraclete Press, including the best-selling Living Library series of modernized classic texts; A Voice from the Monastery—giving voice to men and women monastics about what it means to live a spiritual life today; award-winning literary faith fiction; and books that explore Judaism and Islam and discover how these faiths inform Christian thought and practice.

Recordings

From Gregorian chant to contemporary American choral works, our music recordings celebrate the richness of sacred choral music through the centuries. Paraclete is proud to distribute the recordings of the internationally acclaimed choir Gloriæ Dei Cantores, who have been praised for their "rapt and fathomless spiritual intensity" by *American Record Guide*, and the Gloriæ Dei Cantores Schola, which specializes in the study and performance of Gregorian chant. Paraclete is also the exclusive North American distributor of the recordings of the Monastic Choir of St. Peter's Abbey in Solesmes, France, long considered to be a leading authority on Gregorian chant performance.

Learn more about us at our Web site:
www.paracletepress.com, or call us toll-free at
1-800-451-5006.

Also from Paraclete Press

Mudhouse Sabbath
By Lauren Winner

Lauren invites Christians to enrich their faith with eleven spiritual practices from Judaism. Whether discussing attentive eating, candle-lighting, or the differences between the Jewish Sabbath and a Sunday spent at the *Mudhouse*, her favorite coffee shop, Winner writes with appealing honesty and rare insight.

ISBN: 978-1-55725-532-7, $14.95, Paperback

Radical Hospitality
By Lonni Collins Pratt and
Fr. Dan Homan

Deep within the heart of Benedictine spirituality lies a remedy to hatred, fear, and suspicion: hospitality. Sharing monastic wisdom as well as stories from their own lives, Pratt and Homan encourage us to embrace the true meaning of hospitality, by welcoming the stranger—not only into our homes, but into our hearts.

ISBN: 978-1-55725-441-2, $16.95, Paperback

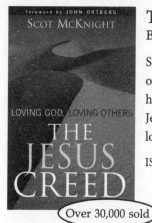